TEATIME AT GROSVENOR SQUARE

TEATIME AT GROSVENOR SQUARE

AN UNOFFICIAL COOKBOOK FOR FANS OF *BRIDGERTON*

75 Sinfully Delectable Recipes

DAHLIA CLEARWATER

Skyhorse Publishing

Skyhorse Publishing books may be purchased in bulk at special discounts for sales promotion, corporate gifts, fund-raising, or educational purposes. Special editions can also be created to specifications. For details, contact the Special Sales Department, Skyhorse Publishing, 307 West 36th Street, 11th Floor, New York, NY 10018 or info@skyhorsepublishing.com.

Skyhorse® and Skyhorse Publishing® are registered trademarks of Skyhorse Publishing, Inc.®, a Delaware corporation.

Visit our website at www.skyhorsepublishing.com.

10 9 8 7 6 5 4 3 2

Library of Congress Cataloging-in-Publication Data is available on file.

Cover design by Brian Peterson and Melissa Gerber
Cover photograph by Heather Barnes via Unsplash
Interior design by Chris Schultz
All recipe photos used by permission of Shutterstock.com

Print ISBN: 978-1-5107-6729-4
eBook ISBN: 978-1-5107-6803-1

Printed in China

CONTENTS

WELCOME TO GROSVENOR SQUARE

You are cordially invited to *Teatime at Grosvenor Square*. The spectacle, luxury, and tantalizing saga of *Bridgerton* has captured the hearts and imaginations of millions of viewers. But among all the heart-racing drama and Regency finery, one thing truly stands out: the magnificent food. Spectacular cakes, candy-colored cookies, fresh fruit as far as the eye can see—it's enough to make even Lady Whistledown's wearied mouth water!

Unlike the ladies of *le bon ton*, you probably don't have a staff whipping up elaborate dishes for you at the wave of a hand. (Or do you?) You can, however, make many of these delectable treats yourself, which Eloise might argue is even better. After all, is there a more worthy endeavor than delighting friends (and upstaging adversaries) with luscious treats?

Let *Teatime at Grosvenor Square* be your guide to dining like society's finest. Create a proper afternoon tea complete with finger sandwiches and flavorful sweets. Impress worthy suitors with traditional cocktails and savory roasts. Or just indulge in the best food that *Bridgerton* has to offer while binge-watching the sumptuous fun again and again!

CHAPTER ONE
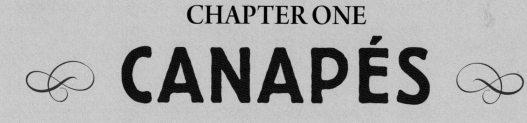
CANAPÉS

HONEYED FIG CROSTINI

Decadence and gorgeous fresh fruit are two things the *ton* and this canapé have in spades. And much like *Bridgerton*, these crostini offer a mouthwatering balance of salty and sweet.

YIELDS 8

1 large baguette

2 tablespoons extra-virgin olive oil

½ cup ricotta cheese

8 medium figs, sliced

1 tablespoon honey

Freshly ground black pepper

1 tablespoon chopped fresh mint leaves

1. Place a rack in the center of the oven and preheat it to 350°F. Line a large, rimmed baking sheet with parchment paper.
2. Slice the baguette into roughly eight 1-inch slices and arrange them on the prepared baking sheet. Brush each slice with oil.
3. Bake the bread until golden, 8–10 minutes, then remove it from the oven and allow it to cool on the baking sheet for 5 minutes.
4. To assemble the crostini, spread ricotta cheese over each slice of bread and top it with the fig slices, a drizzle of honey, a bit of black pepper, and some fresh mint for garnish.

SALMON AND AVOCADO PROFITEROLES

This is a canapé worthy of the Viscount Bridgerton (and just a little reminiscent of his incredible twist of hair). Smoked salmon and creamy avocado complement each other beautifully in a whisp of delicate pastry.

YIELDS 24

1 cup water

½ cup unsalted butter

1 teaspoon sugar

Kosher salt

1 cup sifted all-purpose flour

1 teaspoon baking powder

3 large eggs

2 medium avocados

Juice of 1 lime

1 pinch cayenne pepper

6 ounces smoked salmon

Pea shoots, for garnish

1. Preheat the oven to 400°F and line two baking sheets with parchment paper.
2. In a heavy-bottomed saucepan over medium-high heat, bring the water, butter, sugar, and a pinch of salt to a low boil. Stir until the butter melts completely.
3. Stir in the flour and baking powder until well combined. The dough is ready when it begins to pull away from the pan. Remove it from the heat and transfer it to a large bowl.
4. Using a hand mixer on medium speed, beat the dough for 1 minute to allow it to cool. Then mix in the eggs, one at a time, stopping to scrape down the sides of the bowl using a spatula. The dough should be thick, smooth, and glossy.
5. Using your hands, create 24 dough balls, each one roughly 1½ inches across. Place them 2 inches apart on the prepared baking sheets.
6. Bake the profiteroles for 10 minutes, then reduce the heat to 350°F and bake for 25 minutes longer, until golden brown. Do not open the oven door during the cooking time or remove the baking sheets until the dough is firm to the touch. Allow the shells to cool before filling.
7. While the profiteroles bake, make the mousse: Pit and peel the avocados and add the flesh to a food processor along with a few pinches of salt; pulse until mashed, about 1 minute.
8. Add the lime juice and cayenne, then process the mixture until smooth, about 2 minutes. Taste and adjust to your liking.
9. Use a serrated knife to cut off the top of each pastry, and remove some of the soft middle. Then use a pastry bag or spoon to fill the middle with the mousse. Top it with a small piece of smoked salmon and place the top back on. Repeat with each profiterole and garnish with pea shoots.

NECTARINE AND GOAT CHEESE TOASTS

This sweet-and-savory canapé is as lovely to look at as it is to eat, making it a worthy addition to any table in the Square. Like Lady Whistledown's gossip, nectarines happen to be at their juiciest during London's social season.

YIELDS 20

½ cup salted butter

10 pieces thinly sliced bread

8 ounces goat cheese

4 large nectarines, pitted and sliced

Honey, for drizzling

Kosher salt

1 handful microgreens, for garnish

1. Preheat the oven to 250°F. Spread a thin layer of butter over both sides of each slice of bread, then use a serrated knife to remove all of the crusts and cut each slice in half. Transfer the slices to a baking sheet.
2. Bake the bread slices for 20 minutes, then flip the bread over and continue baking until golden-brown and crisp, 15–25 minutes.
3. Top each piece of toast with the goat cheese, nectarine slices, a drizzle of honey, and a sprinkling of salt before finishing them with a few microgreens.

CHEESY SUITOR SHRIMP CROSTINI

Some of the *ton*'s suitors lay it on especially thick, like the ones who write love poems for ladies they met just the evening before. Distract them with an equally cheesy appetizer they can enjoy while more serious suitors stake their claim.

YIELDS 16–20

1 pound cooked shrimp

½ cup mayonnaise

2 medium cloves garlic, minced

½ small bunch fresh parsley, chopped, plus
    more for garnish

½ small bunch fresh dill, chopped

1 cup Mexican-blend shredded cheese

2 medium baguettes

1. Preheat the oven to 350°F.
2. Rinse, dry, peel, and coarsely chop the shrimp, then transfer them to a medium bowl. Stir in the mayonnaise, garlic, parsley, dill, and Mexican-blend cheese to create a spread.
3. Slice the baguettes into eight to ten ½-inch slices each, place them on a baking sheet, and divide the mixture evenly among them.
4. Bake the crostini until the cheese has melted and the shrimp are heated through, 8–10 minutes.
5. Serve warm, topped with a bit of parsley and, if serving at a ball, a whole cooked shrimp each.

MUSHROOM AND QUAIL EGG CANAPÉS

Living with your handsome husband in the English countryside has *many* benefits, one of which is the abundance of wild game. Luckily, you can also find quail eggs at your local grocery store and bring a bit of the countryside to you.

YIELDS 12

3 slices white or multigrain bread

4 tablespoons salted butter, divided

8–10 shiitake mushrooms, cleaned, stemmed, and sliced

Kosher salt and freshly ground black pepper

1 small handful fresh basil leaves

½ cup crumbled feta cheese

1 small red onion, sliced

12 quail eggs

1. Lightly toast the bread in a toaster or oven. Then use a small cookie cutter to cut four rounds from each slice of bread and place them on a serving platter. (If you don't have a small cookie cutter to create rounds, simply cut the crusts off the bread and cut each slice into four squares.)

2. Heat a large skillet over medium heat for 5 minutes, then add 2 tablespoons of the butter. When the butter melts and begins to bubble, stir in the mushrooms. Cook, stirring occasionally, until browned, about 10 minutes. Season with salt and pepper to taste, stir again, and transfer the mushrooms to a plate lined with paper towels.

3. To start assembling the canapés, top each toasted round with basil, feta, mushrooms, and onion.

4. Reduce the heat to medium and add the remaining 2 tablespoons butter to the skillet. One at a time, gently crack each quail egg using a knife, drop it into a small bowl, and slide it into the pan. Cook a few eggs at a time until firm, 1–2 minutes each. Season each egg with salt and pepper to taste, and place one on top of each canapé. Enjoy with a knife and fork to avoid any unladylike mishaps.

DILL CREAM CHEESE *VOL-AU-VENTS*

These savory puff pastries have the elegance (and volume) of one of Queen Charlotte's lavish wigs! *Vol-au-vents* are beautiful little pastry bowls that are made easier with a few kitchen items: a 1½-inch round cookie cutter, a 3½-inch round cookie cutter, a wire rack, and a pastry bag.

YIELDS 9

1 sheet frozen puff pastry

1 large egg

1 tablespoon water

6 tablespoons whipped cream cheese

1 tablespoons chopped fresh dill

½ small red pepper, finely diced (optional)

Fresh basil, for garnish

6 ounces smoked salmon (optional)

1. Preheat the oven to 400°F.
2. On a lightly floured surface, gently roll out the sheet of puff pastry until it is ¼ inch thick.
3. Using a 3½-inch round cookie cutter, cut out 18 circles. Then, lightly press a 1½-inch round cookie cutter into the center of half of the pastry circles to mark them, being careful not to cut through them.
4. In a small bowl, whisk together the egg and water to create an egg wash. Brush the pastry rounds with the egg wash, then place the marked rounds on top of the unmarked rounds on a baking sheet.
5. To ensure that the pastry rises uniformly, place your 3½-inch cookie cutter on the sheet between the rounds and place a wire rack on top of the cookie cutter. Bake the pastries for 20–23 minutes, until they are risen and golden.
6. Using the tip of a sharp knife, gently trace the inner circle on each pastry and dig out some of the dough to create a cup for the filling.
7. In a small bowl, combine the whipped cream cheese and chopped dill. Divide the mixture evenly among the pastries, using a spoon to fill each up. Alternatively, you can spoon the filling into a pastry bag with a star tip and pipe it into the cups.
8. Top each golden *vol-au-vent* with red pepper and basil, salmon roses, or both!

AVOCADO MOUSSE CROSTINI

These crostini look the picture of a delicate and delightful canapé, but like a certain Featherington cousin, they'll surprise you with hidden reserves of spiciness. For a milder mousse, use a pepper with a little less heat.

YIELDS 24

3 medium baguettes

Extra-virgin olive oil

Kosher salt and freshly ground black pepper

3 medium ripe avocados, halved, pitted, peeled, and cubed

¼ cup whipping cream

3 tablespoons fresh lime juice

2 teaspoons grated lime zest

1 serrano pepper, seeded and chopped

1 tablespoon chopped fresh cilantro

2 medium cloves garlic, chopped

1 teaspoon sugar

½ teaspoon salt

½ cup crumbled feta cheese (optional)

Edible flowers, for garnish (optional)

1. Preheat the oven to 400°F.
2. Use a serrated knife to cut the baguettes at a slight angle into roughly eight ¼-inch slices each. Brush both sides of each slice with olive oil, place them in a single layer on a baking sheet, and season them with salt and pepper. Bake the crostini until lightly toasted, 7–10 minutes.
3. Remove them from the oven and let them cool on the baking sheet.
4. Add the avocados, cream, lime juice, lime zest, serrano pepper, cilantro, garlic, sugar, and salt to a food processor and process until well combined and smooth.
5. Pipe or spoon 1 tablespoon of the avocado mixture onto each piece of bread and top with a bit of feta, if desired. If you like, add a few edible flowers for that *Bridgerton* touch!

ROASTED VEGETABLE TARTLETS

These colorful tarts would be right at home on the Featherington tea table. You can spoon the cream cheese into the tart shells, but using a piping bag with a star tip will make for a more elegant presentation.

YIELDS 16–20

1 small butternut squash

1 small red onion

Olive oil

Kosher salt and freshly ground black pepper

1 (8-ounce) package cream cheese,
   at room temperature

16–20 premade mini tart shells

1 handful fresh basil leaves, for garnish

Chopped chives, for garnish

1. Preheat the oven to 450°F.
2. Slice the squash and onion into similarly sized half-moons. Add the vegetables to a large bowl, drizzle with olive oil, and season with salt and pepper to taste. Toss them to coat, then spread them in a single layer on a baking sheet.
3. Bake the vegetables until tender and lightly browned, about 15 minutes.
4. To assemble the tartlets, spoon or pipe cream cheese into each shell, top with some of the roasted vegetables, and garnish with basil and chives.

MINI TOMATO PIES

The next time a suitor offers to bring you a bushel of tomatoes, take him up on it and make these delightful tomato tartlets. If you don't have any Gruyère or mozzarella on hand, simply use white cheddar and Monterey Jack (respectively) instead.

YIELDS 16

4 medium plum tomatoes

2 teaspoons kosher salt, divided

1 (17.3-ounce) package frozen puff pastry sheets, thawed

1¼ cups grated Gruyère cheese, divided

½ cup shredded mozzarella cheese, divided

¼ cup mayonnaise

½ teaspoon freshly ground black pepper

½ cup chopped fresh basil, plus whole leaves for garnish

1. Preheat the oven to 375°F.
2. Divide each tomato into approximately eight slices, then lay the slices on paper towels and sprinkle them with 1 teaspoon of the salt. Let them stand for 15 minutes, then flip them onto dry paper towels, sprinkle them with the remaining 1 teaspoon of salt, and let them stand for another 15 minutes. Dab the exposed side of the tomatoes with dry paper towels to soak up any remaining moisture.
3. While the tomatoes dry, prepare the pastry. Roll out the dough on a lightly floured surface. Using a 3- or 3½-inch biscuit cutter, cut eight rounds from each sheet of pastry.
4. Place the pastry rounds into two nonstick muffin pans, pressing the dough flush with the bottom of each cup.
5. Cover the muffin tins with foil and transfer them to the refrigerator until needed.
6. Combine ¾ cup of the Gruyère cheese and ¼ cup of the mozzarella cheese in a small bowl. Stir in the mayonnaise and black pepper until well combined.
7. Divide the cheese mixture evenly among the pastry shells and top each with a tomato slice. Sprinkle each cup with a bit more Gruyère, using about ¼ cup more in total.
8. Divide the chopped basil among the cups and place another tomato slice on each. Transfer the prepared pastries to the oven and bake for 30 minutes.
9. In a small bowl, combine the remaining ¼ cup Gruyère and ¼ cup mozzarella cheese. After the pastries have finished baking, remove them from the oven, top them with the cheese mixture, and continue to bake them until the cheese has melted, 5 minutes more.
10. Allow the tomato pies to cool slightly before serving, garnished with a bit of fresh basil.

SWEET PEA AND LEEK TARTLETS

The secret to a peaceful dinner? Bake the peas into a delicious pastry to avoid anyone launching them across the table. These tartlets are so scrumptious that little ones may actually want to eat their vegetables instead.

YIELDS 12

2 tablespoons unsalted butter

1 cup thinly sliced leeks

1 cup baby sweet peas

1 tablespoon chopped fresh tarragon, plus more for garnish

1 tablespoon chopped fresh parsley

1 (4-ounce) package soft goat cheese, crumbled

1 teaspoon kosher salt

½ teaspoon freshly ground black pepper

3 large eggs, at room temperature and lightly beaten

Nonstick cooking spray

1½ (15-ounce) packages refrigerated piecrusts

1. Melt the butter in a small pan over medium heat, then add the leeks. Let them cook until soft, 6–8 minutes. Stir in the peas, tarragon, and parsley and cook until everything is heated through, 3–4 minutes more. Finally, stir in the goat cheese, salt, and pepper until smooth.

2. Transfer the mixture to a large bowl and let it cool for 15 minutes. Then gently whisk in the eggs until well combined.

3. Preheat the oven to 350°F and prepare twelve 4½ × 2½-inch rectangular tart pans with removable bottoms, spraying each with cooking spray.

4. On a lightly floured surface, gently roll each piecrust into a 12-inch round. Cut each into 6½ × 4½-inch rectangles, gently rerolling the scraps only as necessary. (Don't overwork the dough.) You should have 12 rectangles total.

5. Place the rectangles in the tartlet pans, pressing the dough firmly into the bottoms and up the sides and crimping the edges, if desired. Use a fork to lightly perforate the dough lining the bottoms several times each.

6. Place the tartlet pans on a baking sheet, transfer them to the oven, and bake just until the edges are golden, about 10 minutes.

7. Remove the tartlet shells from the oven and divide the leek filling evenly among them. Then pop them back in the oven and bake until the centers are set, 12–15 minutes.

8. Let the tartlets cool in their pans for 5 minutes before serving, garnished with a sprig of tarragon.

PRIZEWINNING PROSCIUTTO CROSTINI

You don't need Clyvedon Fair's prizewinning pig to whip up this savory treat, but using freshly sliced prosciutto will certainly yield delicious results. For a bit more flavor, consider drizzling these crostini with some balsamic vinegar.

YIELDS 24

3 medium whole-grain baguettes

2 tablespoons extra-virgin olive oil

Kosher salt and freshly ground black pepper

4 ounces cream cheese, at room temperature

⅓ cup crumbled blue cheese

1 pound thinly sliced prosciutto

¼ cup whole walnuts

1 handful fresh basil leaves

1. Preheat the oven to 400°F.
2. Use a serrated knife to cut the baguettes at a slight angle into roughly eight ¼-inch slices each. Brush both sides of each slice with olive oil, place them in a single layer on a baking sheet, and season them with salt and pepper.
3. Bake the slices until lightly toasted, 7–10 minutes. Remove them from the oven and let them cool on the baking sheet.
4. Combine the cream cheese and blue cheese in a small bowl until well blended, and then spread the mixture over the crostini. Finish each with prosciutto, walnuts, and basil.

CLASSIC *GOUGÈRES*

Like Madame Delacroix, these *gougères* sound much more chic than they actually are. In reality, *gougères* are just baked cheese puffs, but they fit in beautifully at a high-society tea. Be warned: Eating these puffs is as addictive as buying new dresses!

YIELDS 24

1 cup water

½ cup unsalted butter

½ teaspoon ground mustard (optional)

½ teaspoon kosher salt

1 cup all-purpose flour

4 large eggs, lightly beaten

1½ cups grated cheese, such as Gruyère
    or Parmesan

1. Arrange two oven racks to divide the oven into equal thirds and preheat the oven to 450°F. Line two baking sheets with silicone baking mats or parchment paper.
2. Add the water, butter, mustard (if using), and salt to a large saucepan over medium-high heat and bring to a boil, stirring to combine.
3. Remove the pan from the heat and stir in the flour to form a soft dough. Then return the pan to the stove over medium-low heat and continue cooking and stirring for 3–5 minutes. The dough should be nutty, glossy, and thick.
4. Transfer the dough to an electric stand mixer preferably fitted with a paddle attachment, or to a bowl with a hand mixer, and beat the dough on medium-low speed for 1 minute, until it cools and is just warm to the touch.
5. Beat in the eggs one at a time, scraping down the sides as needed and ensuring that the dough is smooth between each addition. Then beat in the cheese until the dough is smooth.
6. Scoop 12 rounded tablespoons of dough onto each baking sheet, about 1 inch apart, and bake them for 5 minutes. Then reduce the temperature to 350°F and continue baking for 20–25 minutes longer, until the dough is puffed, deep golden-brown, and dry to the touch. (Swap and rotate the sheets halfway through baking for more even cooking.)
7. Transfer the baking sheets to a wire rack to allow the *gougères* to cool for a few minutes, but serve them while they're still warm. The finished puffs should feel light and hollow.

CRANBERRY BRIE BITES

This sweet-and-savory canapé is as lovely to look at as it is to eat, making it the perfect addition to any table in the Square. Thankfully for busy housekeepers, prepackaged crescent rolls are just as delicious as homemade puff pastry.

YIELDS 24

Nonstick cooking spray

Flour

1 (8-ounce) package crescent roll dough

1 (8-ounce) wheel Brie

½ cup whole-berry cranberry sauce

¼ cup chopped pecans (optional)

6 sprigs rosemary or thyme, cut into
   1-inch pieces

1. Preheat the oven to 375°F and grease a mini muffin pan with cooking spray.
2. On a lightly floured surface, roll out the crescent dough and pinch together the seams.
3. Cut the dough into 24 squares and place one square into each muffin cup.
4. Cut the Brie into small pieces (larger pieces will spill over when cooked) and place one inside each of the dough squares. Top each with a spoonful of cranberry sauce, some chopped pecans (if using), and a small sprig of rosemary.
5. Bake the Brie bites until the pastry is golden, about 15 minutes. Serve hot.

SALMON AND DILL ROSETTES

Bring the florals of *Bridgerton* to your tea table with elegantly decorated salmon rosettes atop whipped lemon-and-dill cream cheese! A piping bag creates a more graceful presentation, but simply spooning the whipped cream cheese onto the toast will do the trick.

YIELDS 6

3 slices pumpernickel or rye bread

4 ounces cream cheese, at room temperature

2 tablespoons finely chopped fresh dill, plus sprigs for garnish

1 pinch salt

1 teaspoon lemon juice

1 teaspoon grated lemon zest, plus more for garnish

3 ounces smoked salmon

1. Toast the bread. Using a 2-inch round cookie cutter, cut 2 rounds from each slice of toast.
2. Using a hand or stand mixer and a large bowl, whip the cream cheese until it is fluffy, 3–5 minutes. Then gently fold in the dill, salt, lemon juice, and lemon zest.
3. Spoon the whipped cream cheese into a piping bag and pipe it onto the toasted rounds.
4. Slice the smoked salmon into small pieces, and roll those pieces into six small rosettes. Place a rosette on each canapé.
5. For an extra touch, garnish with fresh dill and a bit of lemon zest.

PUFF PASTRY SANDWICHES

If White's serves anything besides wine and scotch, it has to be sandwiches like these. With prosciutto, chicken, and coleslaw in delicate puff pastry, they're a cross between a sandwich and a canapé that's both gentlemanly and filling.

YIELDS 18

FOR THE SANDWICHES

2 sheets frozen all-butter puff pastry

1 large egg

1 tablespoon water

1 pound roasted and sliced chicken breast

1 pound thinly sliced prosciutto

Chopped chives, for garnish

FOR THE COLESLAW

⅓ cup mayonnaise

⅓ cup yellow mustard

⅓ cup apple cider vinegar

1 cup sugar, divided, plus more to taste

2 tablespoons hot sauce (optional)

1 teaspoon celery seeds

3½ cups finely shredded green cabbage, patted dry with paper towels

1 large carrot, peeled and grated

⅓ cup kosher salt, plus more to taste

Freshly ground pepper

1. To make the sandwiches, let the puff pastry thaw completely (in the refrigerator overnight works well). Preheat the oven to 400°F. Beat together the egg and water in a small bowl.

2. Carefully unfold the pastry sheets, making sure they don't crack at the seams. (Don't press or roll them or they won't puff up.)

3. Cut the dough into eighteen 3 × 5-inch rectangles, place them on a baking sheet, and brush each with egg wash. Bake them just until they start to puff up and turn golden, about 10 minutes, then reduce the heat to 375°F and continue baking until the pastries are dry, crisp, and deep golden-brown.

4. While the pastries bake, make the coleslaw: In a small bowl, whisk together the mayonnaise, mustard, vinegar, ⅓ cup of the sugar, hot sauce (if using), and celery seeds. In a large bowl, combine the cabbage, carrot, remaining ⅔ cup sugar, and salt and let stand for 5 minutes. Transfer the cabbage mixture to a large colander, rinse it thoroughly under cold water, then dry it thoroughly

using a salad spinner or a baking sheet lined with paper towels. Return the dried cabbage to the large bowl, stir in the dressing, and season with salt, pepper, and sugar to taste.

5. When the pastries have finished baking, let them cool for a few minutes. Then use a serrated knife to slice the tops from the bottoms.

6. Divide the coleslaw, chicken, and prosciutto among the pastry bottoms; sprinkle each with a few chives, and replace the pastry tops before serving to delighted guests.

EGG SALAD FINGER SANDWICHES

You don't have to reinvent the carriage wheel to create a tea-worthy canapé. Even the simplest sandwich will look lovely divided into three and served on a pretty plate. Just be sure to enjoy only one dainty bite at a time, like a lady.

YIELDS 15–20

12 large eggs

½ cup mayonnaise

2 tablespoons chopped fresh chives (optional)

2 tablespoons yellow mustard

Kosher salt and freshly ground black pepper

10 slices multigrain bread

1. Add the eggs and enough water to cover them to a large stockpot, and bring the water to a boil over medium-high heat.
2. Turn off the heat, cover the pot, and let the eggs cook in the hot water for 20 minutes. Then pour out the hot water, replace it with cold water, and let the eggs sit for 5 minutes.
3. Crack and peel the eggs, place them in a plastic bag, and refrigerate them for at least 3 hours, until cold.
4. Finely chop the boiled eggs and add them to a large bowl. Stir in the mayonnaise, chives (if using), mustard, salt, and pepper until combined.
5. Divide the egg salad among five of the bread slices, then top with the remaining five bread slices. Use a serrated knife to cut off all the crusts and slice each sandwich into three thin rectangles or four petite squares.

CLASSIC CUCUMBER SANDWICHES

As much as the Bridgertons like to buck tradition, no afternoon tea would be complete without scrumptious cucumber sandwiches. That doesn't mean you can't play with the flavor a bit. This updated version adds herbs, garlic, and the option of shredded chicken.

YIELDS 30

8 ounces cream cheese, at room temperature

3 tablespoons mayonnaise

2 teaspoons chopped fresh dill

1 teaspoon chopped fresh chives

¼ teaspoon garlic powder

Kosher salt and freshly ground black pepper

1 chicken breast, cooked and
    shredded (optional)

20 slices bread, crusts removed

1 large English cucumber

1 small package microgreens (optional)

1. Add the cream cheese and mayonnaise to a small bowl and use a hand mixer to combine until smooth.
2. Stir in the dill, chives, garlic powder, salt, pepper, and chicken (if using). Spread the mixture over half of the slices of crustless bread.
3. Thinly slice the cucumber and layer the slices in the sandwiches, followed by the microgreens (if using), and the remaining slices of bread. (If you prefer a posh look, layer the cucumbers on top of the sandwiches instead.)
4. Slice each sandwich into three rectangles to create 30 perfectly delicate tea sandwiches.

MORE-THAN-TEA SANDWICHES

≈

If Eloise were a tea sandwich, she would be this one. Although traditional on the surface, the flavor is surprisingly complex—and just a bit tart. Save time for more important endeavors by using canned or shredded rotisserie chicken.

YIELDS 12

3 boneless, skinless chicken breasts

3 tablespoons olive oil

¼ teaspoon dried thyme

Kosher salt and freshly ground black pepper

2 ounces fresh cranberries, finely chopped

1 tablespoon mayonnaise

2 teaspoons Dijon mustard

6 large slices white bread

1 bunch watercress

1 tablespoon unsalted butter

1. Preheat the oven to 350°F.
2. Thoroughly rub the chicken breasts with the olive oil, thyme, salt, and pepper. Place them on a baking sheet and bake for 25–30 minutes, until a meat thermometer inserted into the thickest part reads 165°F. Allow the chicken to cool before using two forks to shred it.
3. In a large bowl, mix together the shredded chicken, cranberries, mayonnaise, mustard, and a pinch of salt.
4. Divide the mixture evenly among three slices of bread. Cover each with watercress.
5. Spread a thin layer of butter on one side of each of the remaining slices of bread and place them buttered-side down to create three sandwiches.
6. Cut off the crusts and slice each sandwich into four rectangular tea sandwiches before serving.

TURKEY AND BRIE TEA SANDWICHES

With blackberry jam and creamy Brie, this creation is as mouthwatering as the Bridgerton men. For a sizzling twist on this tea sandwich, butter both sides of it and toast it until golden in a hot pan.

YIELDS 6

¼ cup blackberry jam

1 small handful baby spinach

6 slices Brie, rind removed

6 ounces sliced turkey breast

4 slices cranberry walnut bread

Balsamic vinaigrette (optional)

1. Divide the jam, spinach, Brie, and turkey breast between two slices of the bread. Drizzle vinaigrette over each, if desired.
2. Top both sandwiches with the remaining bread, then use a serrated knife to remove the crusts and slice each sandwich into three rectangles.

CHAPTER TWO

SCONES AND SPREADS

PROPER ENGLISH SCONES

Mrs. Colson is nothing if not a traditionalist, and she prefers a proper scone for a proper duchess. This recipe results in a beautifully light and fluffy scone—a perfect base for the traditional toppings of jam and clotted cream.

YIELDS 9

2 cups all-purpose flour

4 teaspoons baking powder

½ teaspoon salt

¼ cup sugar

6 tablespoons unsalted butter,
    at room temperature

⅔ cup whole milk

1 large egg

1. Preheat the oven to 425°F and line a baking sheet with parchment paper.
2. Add the flour, baking powder, salt, and sugar to the bowl of a large food processor and pulse to combine. Add the butter and pulse 7–10 times to incorporate it. The mixture should be sandy with no outstanding bits of butter. Transfer the mixture to a large bowl.
3. In a small bowl, whisk together the milk and egg. Reserve 2 tablespoons of it for the egg wash and pour the rest into the large bowl with the dry ingredients.
4. Use a spatula to combine the wet and dry ingredients until a rough dough forms, then transfer the dough to a lightly floured surface.
5. Knead the dough just until it comes together and forms a relatively smooth ball. (Be careful not to overwork the dough.)
6. Using your hands, gently pat the dough out to about 1 inch thick and use a 2½-inch biscuit cutter to cut out seven rounds. Gently pat the scraps together and cut out two more rounds.
7. Place the rounds onto the prepared baking sheet, leaving a 1-inch space between them, and brush the tops of the dough with the reserved egg wash.
8. Transfer the baking sheet to the oven and bake until the scones are golden-brown and have tripled in height, 13–15 minutes. Enjoy with jam (see page 51) and clotted cream (see page 49)!

REGENCY RAISIN SCONES

These are the scones Mrs. Colson would allow after a year of Daphne's softening influence. Still a traditional Regency treat, raisin scones are just a bit more indulgent than the original. But only *a bit*.

YIELDS 18–24

5 cups all-purpose flour

2 tablespoons baking powder

½ cup sugar, plus more for topping

½ teaspoon salt

¾ cup (1½ sticks) cold, unsalted butter, chopped

1¾ cups buttermilk, plus more for brushing

2 large eggs

¾ cup raisins

1. Move the racks to the middle of the oven, preheat it to 375°F, and line two baking sheets with parchment paper.
2. Whisk together the flour, baking powder, sugar, and salt in a large bowl. Add the chopped butter and continue whisking until the bits of butter are pea sized.
3. In a small bowl, whisk together the buttermilk and eggs. Whisk the buttermilk mixture into the dry ingredients just until combined. Be careful not to overmix.
4. Transfer the rough dough onto a lightly floured surface, sprinkle the raisins over it, and knead just until the loose flour is absorbed. Using your hands, pat the dough out until it is about 1 inch thick. Use a 2½-inch biscuit cutter to cut out 18–24 rounds, gently gathering the scraps and cutting out as needed until you use all of the dough.
5. Transfer the rounds to the baking sheets, leaving a 1-inch space between them. Brush the tops of the scones with buttermilk and then sprinkle them lightly with sugar.
6. Transfer the baking sheets to the oven and bake the scones for 15–20 minutes, swapping the trays after 10 minutes, until they are risen and golden-brown. (Perfectly baked scones will sound hollow when tapped on the bottom.)

CHERRY SCONES

Knowing that her mistress likes to change things up, Rose would certainly opt for a more modern scone. The bright and cheerful flavor of cherry suits the Bridgerton family's joyful approach to dining.

YIELDS 8

15–20 fresh cherries

3¾ cups all-purpose flour

2 teaspoons baking powder

1 pinch salt

⅓ cup granulated sugar

⅓ cup unsalted butter

¾ cup + 2 tablespoons milk

2 medium eggs

1–2 tablespoons brown sugar (optional)

1. Preheat the oven to 460°F and line a baking sheet with parchment paper.
2. Pit and roughly chop the cherries and set them aside.
3. Sift the flour, baking powder, and salt into a large bowl and gently stir in the granulated sugar.
4. Roughly chop the butter and use a pastry blender or a fork to cut in the butter until the mixture is crumbly. Stir in the chopped cherries.
5. In a small bowl, whisk together the milk and eggs. Reserve 2 tablespoons of it for the egg wash and pour the rest into the large bowl with the dry ingredients.
6. Use a spatula to combine the wet and dry ingredients until a soft dough forms, then transfer the dough to a lightly floured surface. Use your hands to shape it into a large round, about 9 inches across and 1 inch think.
7. Cut the dough into eight wedges using a floured knife, and transfer the wedges to the prepared baking sheet. Brush the wedges with the reserved egg wash and sprinkle them with the brown sugar, if desired.
8. Transfer the baking sheet to the oven and bake until the scones are golden-brown, about 12 minutes. Move them to a wire rack to cool before serving.

CRANBERRY ORANGE SCONES

When you've had enough tradition, learn from Benedict to enjoy all the flavor that life and scones have to offer! Like a Granville party, this recipe is a little "nutty." But the scones are plenty flavorful without the pecans, if you prefer.

YIELDS 10

Nonstick cooking spray

1 cup dried cranberries

½ cup chopped pecans (optional)

¼ cup + 1 tablespoon orange juice, divided

¼ cup half-and-half

1 large egg, at room temperature

2 cups all-purpose flour

1 tablespoon grated orange zest

2 teaspoons baking powder

½ teaspoon kosher salt

¼ teaspoon baking soda

10 teaspoons granulated sugar, divided

⅓ cup cold unsalted butter

1 tablespoon whole milk

½ cup powdered sugar

1. Preheat the oven to 400°F. Grease a baking sheet.
2. Combine the cranberries, pecans (if using), ¼ cup of the orange juice, the half-and-half, and the egg in a medium bowl and set the mixture aside.
3. In a large bowl, stir together the flour, orange zest, baking powder, salt, baking soda, and 7 teaspoons of the granulated sugar. Use a pastry blender or a fork to cut in the butter until the mixture is crumbly.
4. Stir the cranberry mixture into the flour mixture until a soft dough forms. Gently knead the dough 6–8 times on a lightly floured surface, then pat it into an 8-inch circle. Cut the dough into 10 even wedges.
5. Separate the wedges and place them on the prepared baking sheet. Brush each one with the milk and sprinkle them with the remaining 7 teaspoons of granulated sugar. Bake the scones for 12–15 minutes until they are lightly browned, then move them to a wire rack to cool.
6. In a small bowl, mix together the powdered sugar and remaining 1 tablespoon of orange juice, adding more sugar to thicken the glaze or more juice to thin it. Drizzle it over the scones before serving them warm.

SECRETLY SWEET SCONES

Like Simon Basset, these scones have hidden depths of sweetness. You don't need to be quite as unyielding as the duke, though. Let your personality shine through by choosing three different flavors for these fruit-filled scones.

YIELDS 18

2¼ cups all-purpose flour

½ teaspoon salt

¼ cup granulated sugar

1 tablespoon baking powder

6 tablespoons cold unsalted butter, chopped

2 large eggs, beaten

⅓ cup milk, plus more for brushing

1 teaspoon pure vanilla extract

1–1½ cups favorite jam or spread

2 tablespoons coarse sugar, for sprinkling

1. Preheat the oven to 375°F and line a baking sheet with parchment paper.
2. Whisk together the flour, salt, granulated sugar, and baking powder in a large bowl. Use a pastry blender or a fork to cut in the butter until the mixture is crumbly.
3. In a small bowl, combine the eggs, milk, and vanilla. Use a spatula to incorporate the wet ingredients into the dry ingredients until a soft dough forms.
4. Divide the dough into three equal pieces, and form each piece into a disk about 4 inches across and 1 inch thick.

Place the dough on a second baking sheet and transfer the sheet to the freezer for 30 minutes.

5. Using a large, serrated knife, slice each chilled round in half horizontally, removing the top from the bottom. (Use a gentle sawing motion, slice to the middle of the disk, then turn the disk and slice from the other side until you reach your first cut.)
6. Spread the bottom half of each disk with your preferred jam, then replace the tops and press down gently.
7. Move the rounds to the prepared baking sheet, brush each with milk, and sprinkle each with the coarse sugar. Transfer the baking sheet to the oven and bake until the scones are golden-brown and a toothpick inserted into the center of each comes out dry, about 28 minutes.
8. Remove the baking sheet from the oven and set it on a cooling rack for 10 minutes. Cut each disk into six wedges and serve warm.

CREAM TEA SCONES

One look at the creamy colors of *Bridgerton* and you instantly feel lighter. These scones are the embodiment of that feeling. Using cream instead of butter not only gives you fluffier scones, but it also creates a little less work for you.

YIELDS 12

3 cups all-purpose flour

1 tablespoon baking powder

1 teaspoon salt

¼–⅓ cup granulated sugar

1 teaspoon pure vanilla extract

1⅓–1½ cups heavy or whipping cream, plus more for brushing

Coarse sugar, for topping

1. Preheat the oven to 425°F and line a baking sheet with parchment paper.
2. In a large bowl, whisk together the flour, baking powder, salt, and granulated sugar. In a small bowl, combine the vanilla with 1⅓ cups of the cream. Slowly fold the wet mixture into the dry ingredients just until combined, adding more cream as needed (up to 3 tablespoons) to form a soft dough and incorporate all of the flour.
3. Divide the dough in half and transfer it to a lightly floured surface. Gently pat each half into a round roughly 5½ inches across and ¾ inch thick.
4. Brush each round with heavy cream, and top with a sprinkling of coarse sugar.
5. Move the rounds to the prepared baking sheet and cut each into six wedges. Pull the wedges apart until you have about 1 inch of space between each wedge.
6. Put the baking sheet in the freezer for 15 minutes.
7. Transfer the chilled scones to the oven and bake them for 14–15 minutes, until golden-brown and a toothpick inserted into the center of each comes out dry. Serve warm with an array of beautiful toppings.

SILKY CLOTTED CREAM

Much like Lady Danbury—who some might say is the true queen of the *ton*—clotted cream seems daunting but is actually delightful. Creating the sweet, nutty cream is a two-day process, but most of that is hands-off.

SERVES 16

4 cups heavy cream
   (avoid ultra-pasteurized, if possible)

1. In the morning, preheat the oven to 175–180°F. Pour the cream into a shallow 8- or 9-inch baking dish so that it is roughly 1½–2 inches deep.
2. Transfer the dish to the oven and bake the cream for 12 hours, undisturbed.
3. Carefully remove the dish from the oven and let the cream cool to room temperature. Then cover it with plastic wrap and refrigerate it overnight.
4. Lift a corner of the top layer of thickened cream and carefully pour off the liquid underneath it. (You can reserve this to use in baking scones.)
5. Transfer the thickened (clotted) cream into a small bowl or jar. Clotted cream can be stored in the refrigerator, covered, for up to 5 days.

BOLD RASPBERRY JAM

Take Eloise's advice and be bold! The flavor of this jam is just a bit brighter than most store-bought varieties thanks to its simplified ingredients. This small batch should be just enough for teatime, but you can double it and preserve the results, if you like.

SERVES 16

1 cup sugar

2 cups fresh raspberries

1. Preheat the oven to 250°F.
2. Pour the sugar into a shallow baking pan and warm it in the oven for 15 minutes.
3. Meanwhile, add the berries to a large saucepan and bring them to a boil over high heat, using a potato masher to mash them as they cook. Then boil them for 1 minute more, stirring constantly.
4. Stir in the warm sugar, return the mixture to a boil, and continue cooking until it forms a gel, about 5 minutes.
5. Use a cold spoon to check that the jam is finished: Dip it into the hot jam and immediately lift it out and turn it horizontally. The jam should be thick and run together before falling off the spoon.
6. Pour the finished jam into a lovely serving bowl. Store excess in the refrigerator or properly preserve it.

SWEET ORANGE MARMALADE

Ripe fruit festoons every food-laden table in *Bridgerton*'s London, but there's more than one way to include it in your own celebrations. Freshly made orange marmalade is a staple in English breakfasts, teas, and sweets.

SERVES 24

5 pounds ripe oranges

6 cups sugar

4 cups water

3 sterilized pint jars with sealable lids

1. Wash and dry the fruit. Then, using a sharp vegetable peeler or paring knife, remove the brightly colored zest from the fruit, being sure to avoid the white pith beneath it.

2. Slice the zest into thin, 1-inch-long strips. Then cut the ends off the zested fruit and carefully cut the white pith from around each piece.

3. Working over a large bowl, use a sharp knife to remove the orange segments from the membranes holding them together. Squeeze any remaining juice from the membranes and set them aside with the seeds.

4. Combine the zest, fruit, juice, sugar, and water in a large, heavy pot and bring to a boil over medium-high heat. Stir just until the sugar dissolves, then stop stirring and let the mixture cook while you create the pectin bag.

5. Meanwhile, add the membranes and seeds to the center of a double layer of cheesecloth. Lift up the corners and tie the cheesecloth into a bag around them. (This bag helps the marmalade gel.)

6. Add the bag to the pot and bring the mixture to a boil. Let the marmalade boil until it reaches 220°F on a candy thermometer, then hold it there for 5 minutes without stirring.

7. Use a cold spoon to check that the jam is finished: Dip it into the hot jam and immediately lift it out and turn it horizontally. The jam should be thick and run together before falling off the spoon.

8. Lift the bag from the pot, squeeze any excess marmalade back into the pot (be careful—the bag will be hot), and discard the bag. Remove the marmalade from the heat and let it sit for 5 minutes.

9. Stir the marmalade one last time, then ladle it into the jars, leaving ½ inch of headspace at the top of each. Closed and in the refrigerator, the marmalade will keep for up to 4 weeks.

LUSCIOUS LEMON CURD

Like a newsletter hot off the presses from Lady Whistledown's secret printer, this lemon curd is both tart and refreshing. You can use it as a spread for your scones or even as the main event in a dessert like the Lemonade Tartlets on page 89.

SERVES 12

3 large lemons

1½ cups sugar

½ cup unsalted butter, at room temperature

4 extra-large eggs

⅛ teaspoon kosher salt

1. Using a vegetable peeler or paring knife, remove the zest from the lemons, being careful to avoid the white pith. Squeeze the lemons to make ½ cup of juice. Set the juice aside.
2. Add the lemon zest and the sugar to the bowl of a food processor and pulse until the zest is very finely minced and combined with the sugar.
3. Using a hand or stand mixer, cream the butter in a large bowl. Beat in the sugar mixture, eggs (one at a time), salt, and lemon juice and continue mixing until everything is well combined.
4. Pour the mixture into a 2-quart saucepan. Cook and stir it over low heat until it thickens, about 10 minutes, then remove it from the heat. Ladle some of the lemon curd into a serving dish and the rest into an airtight container and refrigerate until ready to enjoy it.

BLACKBERRY WHIPPED CREAM

With its lovely wisteria color, this delicious whipped cream is a must for any *Bridgerton*-themed tea. It makes a tasty companion to Cream Tea Scones (page 47), a surprising filling for Profiteroles (page 65), and an indulgent topping to any trifle (pages 79 and 92).

SERVES 16

FOR THE SEEDLESS BLACKBERRY JAM

5 cups fresh blackberries

2 cups granulated sugar

1–2 tablespoons lemon juice (optional)

FOR THE WHIPPED CREAM

1 cup heavy whipping cream

1 tablespoon powdered sugar

¼ cup seedless blackberry jam

1. To make the blackberry jam, place the blackberries in a large saucepan, bring to a boil over medium-high heat, and cook for 10 minutes. Mash them well and strain them through a fine-mesh sieve or jelly bag.
2. Return the fruit to the pan over medium-low heat and stir in the granulated sugar and lemon juice (if using). Let the jam simmer, stirring occasionally, until it gels, about 20 minutes.
3. Use a cold spoon to check that the jam is finished: Dip it into the hot jam and immediately lift it out and turn it horizontally. The jam should be thick and run together before falling off the spoon.
4. Store excess jam in the refrigerator.
5. To make the whipped cream, add the cream and powdered sugar to a large, chilled bowl. Use a hand or stand mixer to beat the ingredients until they form stiff peaks. Then, beat in the blackberry jam on low speed until just combined.
6. Serve the blackberry whipped cream in a serving bowl alongside scones and pastries, or use a pastry bag fitted with a star tip to elegantly pipe it into the sweets.

PERFECT PAIR ORANGE BUTTER

Of all the people in *Bridgerton*, Will Mondrich might be the most lucky in love. Alice is a true partner in their happy and hard-won marriage. For an even sweeter union, replace the orange zest in this recipe with some of the Sweet Orange Marmalade on page 53.

SERVES 8

1 large orange

6 tablespoons unsalted butter, at room temperature

1 tablespoon powdered sugar

1 dash cinnamon (optional)

1. Zest the orange using a citrus zester or Microplane, then juice the orange to produce just 1 tablespoon of juice.
2. Add the zest, juice, butter, powdered sugar, and cinnamon (if using) to a small bowl and use a hand mixer or whisk to blend everything until the mixture is well combined.
3. Transfer the butter to an appropriate serving dish or container and refrigerate until needed.

CINNAMON HONEY BUTTER

Need a quick and easy upgrade to elevate your nibbles into royalty-worthy fare? This simple recipe takes just a little forethought and results in an effortlessly decadent addition to your scones or muffins.

SERVES 10

1 cup unsalted butter, at room temperature

½ cup honey

1 teaspoon ground cinnamon

1. Add the butter, honey, and cinnamon to a small bowl and use a hand mixer or whisk to blend them until well combined.
2. Transfer the butter to an appropriate serving dish and refrigerate until needed.

CHAPTER THREE

TEATIME SWEETS

RED CURRANT QUEEN CAKES

Queen Charlotte's tastes run a little more refined than these simple sugar-dusted cakes can satisfy, but they are a true Regency classic. The brightness of the currants coupled with the cake's light and crumby consistency will quickly make these a favorite in your home, too.

YIELDS 12

1½ cups all-purpose flour

1 teaspoon baking powder

1 pinch kosher salt

½ cup unsalted butter

⅔ cup powdered sugar, plus more for dusting

2 large eggs

Zest of 1 medium lemon

1 teaspoon pure vanilla extract

½ cup red currants

2 tablespoons milk (optional)

1. Preheat the oven to 350°F and prepare a muffin pan with liners.
2. Combine the flour, baking powder, and salt in a large bowl.
3. In another large bowl, cream together the butter and sugar using a hand mixer until it becomes light and fluffy.
4. Mix in the eggs one at a time, then mix in the lemon zest and vanilla.
5. Sift the dry ingredients into the butter mixture, use a spatula to stir the two together until combined, then gently fold in the currants. If the batter seems too thick, stir in the milk, 1 tablespoon at a time.
6. Spoon the batter into the prepared muffin cups and bake the cakes for 15–20 minutes until the cakes are golden and a toothpick inserted into the center comes out dry.
7. Remove the cakes from the oven, allow them to cool for 5 minutes, then dust with powdered sugar and serve warm.

PROFITEROLES (CLASSIC CREAM PUFFS)

Even a reluctant Eloise might entertain a suitor if he brought her a few of these sweet treats. For a lavender touch that's right at home in the Bridgerton drawing room, fill them with the Blackberry Whipped Cream on page 56.

YIELDS 28

For the Pastry

½ cup water

½ cup whole milk

½ cup unsalted butter

1 teaspoon granulated sugar

¼ teaspoon salt

1 cup all-purpose flour

4 large eggs, at room temperature

For the Cream

2 cups heavy whipping cream, chilled

¼ cup granulated sugar

1 teaspoon pure vanilla extract

Powdered sugar, for dusting

1. Move a rack to the center of the oven and preheat the oven to 425°F. Line a rimmed baking sheet with parchment paper.

2. To make the pastry, in a medium saucepan, combine the water, milk, butter, granulated sugar, and salt. Bring the mixture just to a boil over medium heat, then remove it from the heat and stir in the flour until fully incorporated.

3. Transfer the pan back to the stove over medium heat and stir for 1½–2 minutes, until the dough comes together to form a smooth ball.

4. Transfer the dough to a large bowl. Use a hand mixer on medium speed to beat it for 1 minute, allowing it to cool. Mix in the eggs one at a time, allowing each to fully incorporate before adding the next. Continue mixing for 1 more minute until the dough is smooth and forms a thick ribbon when you shut off the mixer and pull the beaters up.

5. Transfer the dough to a piping bag fitted with a ½-inch round tip. Pipe 28 mounds onto the prepared baking sheet, 1 inch apart and each one measuring about 1½ inches in diameter and ½ inch tall.

6. Bake the profiteroles for 10 minutes in the center of the oven, then lower the temperature to 325°F and bake until the pastries are golden-brown on top, 20–22 minutes longer. Transfer the puffs to a wire rack to cool completely.

7. To make the whipped cream, beat together the cream, granulated sugar, and vanilla on medium-high speed until the cream is fluffy and forms stiff peaks. Transfer it to a piping bag fitted with a large open star tip.

8. Pipe the cream into the cooled profiteroles (by pushing the star tip in or slicing the tops off), dust them with powdered sugar, and serve.

MERINGUE KISSES

These kisses taste sinful, but they won't ruin your family's honor if you sneak a few in the garden. Divide the batter into batches before adding food coloring if you want kisses in multiple colors. They won't keep for long, so seize the moment and enjoy them while you can.

YIELDS 60

4 large eggs

¼ teaspoon cream of tartar

¼ teaspoon kosher salt

¾ cup sugar

½ teaspoon pure vanilla extract

1–2 drops gel food coloring (optional)

1. Preheat the oven to 200°F and line two large baking sheets with parchment paper.
2. Very carefully separate the eggs and place the whites in a large mixing bowl, ensuring that they are completely free of yolk. (Discard the yolks or save them for other recipes.) Add the cream of tartar and salt to the bowl.
3. Using a hand or stand mixer, whip the egg whites on medium speed until the mixture is foamy and just beginning to turn white.
4. Continue to whip, adding in the sugar very slowly, about ¼ teaspoon at a time. Then increase the mixer's speed to high and whip until the meringue is glossy and very stiff.
5. Mix in the vanilla, then remove the mixer and use a spatula to gently fold in the food coloring, if using.
6. Transfer the meringue to a piping bag fitted with a French star tip and pipe sixty 1-inch kisses onto the prepared baking sheets.
7. Transfer the baking sheets to the oven and bake the meringues for 2–2½ hours, until light and crisp but not browned. Enjoy them immediately!

TOWER-WORTHY MACARONS

Every ball in *Bridgerton* seems to feature a tower of these tasty French treats, and for good reason: They're as lovely as they are delectable. To make multiple colors at once, simply divide the batter before adding your food coloring.

YIELDS 30

FOR THE MACARONS

1¾ cups powdered sugar

1 cup finely ground almond flour

1 teaspoon salt, divided

3 egg whites, at room temperature

¼ cup granulated sugar

½ teaspoon pure vanilla extract

2 drops gel food coloring

FOR THE FILLING

1 cup unsalted butter, at room temperature

3 cups powdered sugar

1 teaspoon pure vanilla extract

3 tablespoons heavy cream

1. To make the macarons, add the powdered sugar, almond flour, and ½ teaspoon of the salt to the bowl of a large food processor and process on low speed until the mixture is very fine. Then sift it through a fine-mesh sieve into a large bowl.

2. In another large bowl, use a hand or stand mixer to whip the egg whites and remaining ½ teaspoon of salt on medium speed until soft peaks form. Slowly beat in the granulated sugar, about ¼ teaspoon at a time, until it's fully incorporated and stiff peaks form, then beat in the vanilla.

3. Using a spatula, gently fold in the food coloring just until combined. Then fold in the sifted flour mixture a third at a time. Continue gently folding the batter until it becomes stiff enough that you can lift the spatula and make a ribbon figure eight.

4. Spoon the macaron batter into a piping bag fitted with a round tip. Pipe four dots of batter in each corner of two rimmed baking sheets, and line the sheets with parchment paper, pressing it into the dots to keep the paper in place.

5. Pipe sixty 1½-inch circles about 2 inches apart onto the prepared baking sheets, then tap the baking sheets on a flat surface several times to release any bubbles in the batter. Let the macarons sit at room temperature for up to 1 hour, until dry to the touch, and preheat the oven to 300°F.

6. Transfer the baking sheets to the oven and bake the macarons for 17 minutes, swapping the baking sheets midway through, until they're well risen and not sticking to the parchment paper, then transfer them to a wire rack to cool completely.

7. Meanwhile, make the filling: Place the butter in another large bowl and use a hand or stand mixer to beat the butter until light and fluffy. Sift in the powdered sugar and beat until the mixture is fully creamed. Beat in the vanilla, then beat in the cream, 1 tablespoon at a time, until it's fully incorporated.

8. Spoon the filling into a second piping bag fitted with a round tip. Pipe a bit of filling on the flat bottom of a macaron shell and top it with another macaron, bottom-side down. Repeat with the remaining shells and filling.

9. Move the finished macarons to an airtight container to set for 24 hours before enjoying (or displaying in a grand tower).

CINNAMON MACARONS WITH BRANDY BUTTERCREAM

Like most Regency-era Londoners, the good people of the *ton* like their liquor as much as they like their sweets. Thanks to a delicious brandy buttercream filling, these macarons have the best of both!

YIELDS 30

FOR THE MACARONS

2 cups powdered sugar

1 cup almond flour

¼ teaspoon ground cinnamon

¼ teaspoon ground cloves

¼ teaspoon ground nutmeg

3 egg whites

¼ cup granulated sugar

¼ teaspoon cream of tartar

1 pinch kosher salt

FOR THE FILLING

1 cup powdered sugar

¼ teaspoon ground cinnamon

¼ teaspoon ground nutmeg

⅛ teaspoon ground cloves

½ cup unsalted butter, at room temperature

1 teaspoon pure vanilla extract

1 tablespoon brandy

1. Preheat the oven to 350°F and line two baking sheets with parchment paper.
2. To make the macarons, sift the powdered sugar, almond flour, and spices into a large bowl.
3. In another large bowl, use an electric mixer on medium speed to beat the egg whites, granulated sugar, cream of tartar, and salt until foamy. Continue beating the batter on high speed for 5 minutes until medium peaks form.
4. Gently fold in the flour mixture, a third at a time, frequently scraping the bowl. Spoon the batter into a pastry bag fitted with a ½-inch round tip. Pipe sixty 1½-inch circles about 2 inches apart onto the prepared baking sheets.
5. Bake one sheet at a time for 11–12 minutes or until the macarons are set. Let the macarons cool completely before removing them from the parchment paper.
6. To make the filling, combine the powdered sugar and spices in a small bowl. Use an electric mixer on medium speed to cream the butter and vanilla in a large bowl. Gradually beat in the sugar-spice mixture, frequently scraping the bowl. Beat in the brandy until smooth.
7. Spoon the filling into a piping bag fitted with a small round tip. Pipe a bit of buttercream on the flat bottom of a macaron shell and top it with another macaron, bottom-side down. Repeat with the remaining shells and filling.
8. Let the finished macarons set in an airtight container for 24 hours.

RATAFIA BISCUITS FIT FOR BEAUS

When you unexpectedly find yourself named the season's Incomparable, you need to have plenty of biscuits on hand for gentleman callers. These whip up quickly and abundantly. Traditionally, they used ratafia liqueur, but almond extract takes its place nicely.

YIELDS 48

2 egg whites

5 ounces sugar

1 teaspoon almond extract

8 drops rose water (optional)

4 ounces finely ground almonds

2 teaspoons rice flour

1. Preheat the oven to 325°F and line a baking sheet with parchment paper. (Greasing the sheet with butter first can help the parchment stay down.)
2. In a very clean large bowl, use a hand mixer to whip the egg whites just until they're frothy and beginning to turn white.
3. Gradually mix in the sugar, almond extract, rose water (if using), ground almonds, and rice flour. Continue mixing until the batter is thick, smooth, and white.
4. Use a teaspoon dipped in ice water to drop small, ¾-inch mounds onto the parchment paper at least 2 inches apart.
5. Bake the biscuits for 10–12 minutes until golden but not browned, then transfer them to a wire rack to cool. Continue in batches until you have enough for all of your potential suitors!

APRICOT THUMBPRINT COOKIES

Alice Mondrich may not be the muscle in her marriage, but her no-nonsense approach to the *ton's* gossip and business makes her a force to be reckoned with. Like her, these bite-size cookies are both perfectly practical and not at all subtle. They'd also go beautifully with any of the fruit spreads in this book.

YIELDS 46

1 cup unsalted butter, at room temperature

⅔ cup sugar, plus more for rolling

2 large egg yolks, at room temperature

1 teaspoon pure vanilla extract

¼ teaspoon salt

2⅓ cups all-purpose flour, spooned and leveled

½ cup strawberry or apricot jam

1. Preheat the oven to 350°F and line two large baking sheets with parchment paper.

2. Use a hand or stand mixer to cream together the butter and sugar in a large bowl until well combined, 1–2 minutes. Beat in the egg yolks, vanilla, and salt until fully combined, then mix in the flour until the dough comes together.

3. Scoop out the dough by the tablespoon, roll it into balls, roll each ball in sugar (if desired), and place them on the prepared baking sheets. You should get 46 cookies.

4. Press your thumb into each ball of cookie dough to create an indentation, then spoon ½ teaspoon of jam into each.

5. Bake the cookies until they are set and the bottoms are lightly browned, 12–14 minutes.

6. Remove them from the oven and let them cool on the baking sheet for 10 minutes, then transfer the cookies to a wire rack to finish cooling before serving them.

SPARKLING SNOW BALLS

Although Lady Danbury appears dressed almost exclusively in rich jewel tones, her ball is a celebration of frosted hues and the perfect setting for these powdered cookies. They may actually be a bit too poppable for refined events, but a gloved hand will hide the sugary evidence.

YIELDS 72

1 cup unsalted butter, at room temperature

5 tablespoons granulated sugar

2 teaspoons pure vanilla extract

¼ teaspoon salt

2 cups all-purpose flour

2 cups finely chopped walnuts

1½ cups powdered sugar

1. Add the butter and granulated sugar to a large bowl, and use an electric mixer on low speed to cream them together. Mix in the vanilla and salt, then slowly beat in the flour a little at a time. Stir in the nuts. Divide the dough in half, wrapping each half in plastic wrap and refrigerating them both for 45 minutes.

2. Place a rack in the middle of the oven and preheat it to 350°F. Line two baking sheets with parchment paper. Pour the powdered sugar into a small bowl.

3. When the dough is ready, scoop and roll it into seventy-two 1-inch balls.

4. Place the balls on the lined baking sheets, leaving 1–2 inches between them for expansion. Bake for 12–14 minutes, until the cookies are just beginning to brown. (Cracked cookies are a sign of overbaking.)

5. Move the baked cookies to a cooling rack for 2 minutes, then gently roll the still-warm balls in powdered sugar to coat. Let them cool completely on the wire rack before rolling them a second time in the powdered sugar. Store the finished snowballs in an airtight container for up to 4 weeks.

SPICED TEA COOKIES

Siena may be a little beyond the bounds of propriety, but she is the spice of Anthony's otherwise very traditional life. Add a little fire to your own belly with these cinnamon-spiced cookies, which beat bland biscuits any day of the Season.

YIELDS 30

1⅓ cups all-purpose flour

¾ teaspoon ground cinnamon

¼ teaspoon kosher salt

¼ teaspoon baking soda

10 tablespoons unsalted butter,
   at room temperature

1 cup sugar

1 large egg

1 teaspoon pure vanilla extract

1. Preheat the oven to 375°F and line two baking sheets with parchment paper.
2. In a small bowl, sift together the flour, cinnamon, salt, and baking soda. In a large bowl, use an electric mixture on low speed to cream together the butter and sugar, then mix in the egg and vanilla. Stir the dry mixture into the wet one to create the dough.
3. Scoop and roll the dough into thirty 1-inch balls and place them about 2 inches apart on the prepared baking sheets.
4. Bake the cookies for 12–15 minutes, or until they are lightly browned. Let the finished cookies cool before storing them in an airtight container for up to 2 weeks.

CHARMING PECAN TARTLETS

The prince may not have been a love match, but—like these tartlets—he was a wonderful combination of sweetness and warmth. Starting with frozen tart shells allows you to save time, which is especially important if you're whipping up a variety of treats for a royal visit.

YIELDS 12

3 cups chopped pecans

¾ cup sugar

¾ cup dark corn syrup

3 large eggs, lightly beaten

2 tablespoons unsalted butter, melted

1 teaspoon pure vanilla extract

⅛ teaspoon salt

1½ (8-ounce) packages frozen tart shells

1. Preheat the oven to 350°F.
2. Place the pecans in a shallow pan or on a rimmed baking sheet and spread in a single layer. Bake them until toasted and fragrant, 8–10 minutes.
3. Combine the sugar and corn syrup in a medium bowl, then stir in the toasted pecans, eggs, butter, vanilla, and salt.
4. Spoon about ¼ cup of the pecan mixture into each frozen tart shell and place the assembled tarts on a large baking sheet.
5. Bake the tarts until set, 25–30 minutes, then move them to wire racks and let them cool completely, about 30 minutes. These tarts are beautiful when fresh but can also be kept in an airtight container for up to 3 days.

LEMON AND CREAM TRIFLES

Penelope may be sick of yellow, but she surely wouldn't turn her nose up at this sunny lemon treat. Whipped cream tempers some of the brightness—something Pen would probably appreciate in her wardrobe, as well.

SERVES 4

FOR THE PUDDING

2 cups heavy whipping cream

⅔ cup granulated sugar

Finely grated zest of 1 medium lemon

6 tablespoons lemon juice

FOR THE WHIPPED CREAM

1 cup cold heavy whipping cream

2 tablespoons powdered sugar

½ teaspoon pure vanilla extract

1 cup blueberries, for serving

1. To make the pudding, combine the cream, granulated sugar, and lemon zest in a medium saucepan over medium heat. Bring the mixture to a boil. Maintain a gentle boil (lowering the heat if necessary), and cook, stirring frequently, for 5 minutes.

2. Stir in the lemon juice and continue to simmer for 5 more minutes, stirring frequently. Remove the pan from the heat and let the mixture cool for 5 minutes.

3. Strain the mixture through a fine-mesh sieve into a large measuring cup (or other easy-pour container) and put it in the refrigerator, uncovered, until set, 2–3 hours or up to 2 days.

4. To make the whipped cream, using a hand or stand mixer, whip the heavy cream, powdered sugar, and vanilla on medium-high speed until medium-stiff peaks form, 3–4 minutes.

5. Layer into each of four glasses some of the whipped cream, then the lemon pudding, then more whipped cream. Top with blueberries and, if you like, some homemade lemon curd from page 55 and a ratafia biscuit from page 71.

CREAMY VANILLA FLUMMERY

As Daphne discovered at Clyvedon, flummery can be a great help in coaxing gossip out of buttoned-up housekeepers. This updated version (which is still made in a decorative mold) can be eaten as is, served with fresh fruit, or set atop fruit-flavored gelatin as part of an even grander dessert.

SERVES 4–6

Nonstick cooking spray

½ cup cold water

1 (0.25-ounce) envelope unflavored gelatin

1 cup half-and-half

½ cup sugar

1 (8-ounce) package cream cheese,
   at room temperature

1 teaspoon pure vanilla extract

Sliced fresh fruit, for serving (optional)

1. Coat a 4-cup gelatin mold with cooking spray.
2. Add the cold water to a small bowl, then sprinkle in the unflavored gelatin and let it stand for 1 minute.
3. Combine half-and-half and sugar in a small saucepan over medium heat. Cook and stir just until the mixture begins to simmer, then remove it from the heat and stir it into the gelatin until well combined.
4. Using a hand mixer, beat the cream cheese in a large bowl until smooth. Fold in the gelatin mixture, followed by the vanilla.
5. Pour the mixture into the prepared mold and refrigerate it until set but not firm, about 45 minutes. Serve with fresh fruit, if desired.

COFFEE BEAN BLANCMANGE

A coffee-infused dessert like this molded blancmange would certainly have been a more pleasant pick-me-up for Violet Bridgerton than her housekeeper's hangover cure, but nothing beats news of a love match in the Bridgerton household. This recipe uses agar-agar instead of gelatin to give the dish a vegetarian update.

SERVES 6

1⅔ cups coconut cream

¾ cup coconut milk

½ cup coconut sugar

2 teaspoons prepared coffee

2 teaspoons agar-agar

2 tablespoons coffee liqueur

Dark chocolate, for serving

1. In a heavy-bottomed pan, combine the coconut cream, coconut milk, coconut sugar, coffee, and agar-agar over medium heat. Bring the mixture to a boil, whisking, then reduce the heat to low and cook for 5 minutes, stirring often.

2. Stir in the liqueur, then strain the mixture into a small decorative mold and let it cool for 5 minutes. Transfer it to the refrigerator and let the blancmange set overnight.

3. The next day, use a knife to loosen the edges of the dessert. Keeping the mold open-side up, place a platter on top. Carefully flip everything over. If you don't hear the dessert drop, give the mold a firm shake.

4. Serve your beautiful blancmange plain or garnish with dark chocolate and some ratafia-biscuit crumbs (page 71).

RASPBERRY ALMOND MOUSSE

No need to frequent Gunter's Tea Shop for the best treats. This raspberry mousse is as dreamy as the look on Penelope's face when she's thinking of Colin. Or speaking to him. Or looking at him. But maybe not quite as dreamy as when she's dancing with him.

SERVES 6

2 cups fresh raspberries, plus more for
   serving
¾ cup sugar
1 tablespoon unflavored gelatin
3 cups whipping cream
½ teaspoon almond extract
Fresh mint, for garnish

1. Add 2 cups of the raspberries and the sugar to a saucepan over medium heat. Cook, stirring occasionally, until the sugar dissolves, about 5 minutes. Stir in the gelatin until it dissolves, about 1 minute more.
2. Press the raspberry mixture through a fine-mesh sieve to remove the seeds. Chill the mixture for 15 minutes.
3. Meanwhile, add the cream and almond extract to a large bowl. Use a hand or stand mixer to beat the cream on medium speed until stiff peaks form, about 2 minutes.
4. Gently fold the raspberry mixture into the whipped cream until well combined. Divide the mousse among six glasses and let them set in the refrigerator for 1 hour before serving, topped with fresh raspberries and mint.

THREE LADIES FRUIT TARTS

With her three young ladies vying for attention on the marriage market, Lady Featherington seems to have turned to the eye-catching appeal of these gorgeous mixed-fruit tarts for fashion inspiration. An optional apricot-brandy glaze gives the desserts a professional finish (and just a bit of a kick).

YIELDS 16

2 cups whole milk

½ whole vanilla bean, split lengthwise

6 egg yolks

⅔ cup sugar

¼ cup cornstarch

1 tablespoon unsalted butter, cold

½ cup apricot jam

1 tablespoon water

1 tablespoon brandy

16 premade mini tart shells

3 cups assorted fruit slices and berries

1. Add the milk and vanilla bean to a medium saucepan over medium heat and bring to a boil, then turn off the heat and set the mixture aside.

2. In a large bowl, whisk together the egg yolks and sugar until the mixture is light and fluffy. Vigorously whisk in the cornstarch until no lumps remain, then whisk in ¼ cup of the hot milk until incorporated.

3. Whisk in the remaining hot milk, then pour the mixture through a fine-mesh sieve and back into the saucepan.

4. Cook the mixture over medium-high heat, whisking constantly, until thick. Then remove it from the heat and stir in the butter. Pour the custard into a bowl.

5. Let the custard cream cool slightly before covering it with plastic wrap, pressing the plastic lightly against the surface of the custard.

6. Move the custard to the refrigerator to chill for at least 2 hours and up to 24 hours.

7. Remove the custard from the refrigerator 1 hour before assembling the tarts.

8. Stir together the jam, water, and brandy in a small microwavable bowl and microwave it for 30 seconds to warm it. Strain the glaze through a fine-mesh sieve.

9. To assemble the tarts, whisk the custard to loosen it up, then spoon or pipe it into each shell. Top the tarts with the fruit, and then brush the fruit with the glaze for the perfect finishing touch.

LEMONADE TARTLETS

These bright-tasting pastries are just as refreshing as a small glass of lemonade. If you're feeling greedy (or entitled), just take two! The lemon curd in this recipe is a bit sweeter than the one on page 55, but the buttery shortbread crust balances it beautifully.

YIELDS 6

FOR THE PASTRY

½ cup unsalted butter

¼ cup sugar

½ teaspoon pure vanilla extract

1 cup all-purpose flour

¼ teaspoon fine sea salt

FOR THE LEMON CURD

3 large eggs

4 large egg yolks

1 tablespoon grated lemon zest

¾ cup fresh lemon juice

¾ cup sugar

¼ teaspoon fine sea salt

½ cup unsalted butter, cubed

Fresh berries, for serving (optional)

1. To make the pastry, using a hand or stand mixer and a large bowl, cream together the butter and sugar. Mix in the vanilla, then mix in the flour and salt until well combined. Refrigerate the dough for 30 minutes.

2. Preheat the oven to 300°F. Remove the dough from the refrigerator and press it into six mini tart pans. Place the pans on a baking sheet and bake the tart shells until lightly golden, 10–15 minutes. Remove the shells from the oven and let them cool before removing them from the pans.

3. Meanwhile, to make the lemon curd, whisk together the eggs and egg yolks in a large bowl until well combined and set the bowl aside.

4. Add the lemon zest, juice, sugar, and salt to a medium saucepan over medium heat and cook, stirring, until the sugar dissolves. Turn off the heat and slowly whisk the mixture into the eggs, ½ cup at a time.

5. Pour the mixture back into the pan over low heat and continue whisking constantly until it thickens, about 5 minutes.

6. Remove the curd from the heat and stir in the cubed butter until well combined. Strain the curd through a fine-mesh sieve to remove the zest and put it in the refrigerator to chill for 30 minutes.

7. Once chilled, spoon the curd into the tart shells, top with berries (if you like), and enjoy!

SINFUL VANILLA ICE CREAM

Only Simon Basset could turn something as innocent as vanilla ice cream into an effortless act of seduction. The custard base in this recipe results in a creaminess that will make you want to lick the spoon clean—or watch someone else do it.

SERVES 6

1 cup whole milk

4 large egg yolks

½ cup sugar

1 cup heavy cream

2 teaspoons pure vanilla extract or vanilla bean paste

1. Add the milk to a small saucepan and bring it to a simmer over medium-low heat without stirring.
2. Whisk together the egg yolks and sugar in another, medium saucepan until the mixture is light yellow in color and well combined. Then gradually pour in the warm milk, stirring constantly.
3. Bring the mixture to 165°F over medium heat, never allowing it to boil, then immediately remove it from the heat.
4. Transfer the custard to an airtight container and put it in the refrigerator to chill for at least 2 hours, preferably overnight.
5. Once the custard base is at 65°F, it's ready. Stir in the heavy cream and vanilla, then pour the ice cream mixture into your ice cream maker and process it according to the manufacturer's instructions.

TRADITIONAL ENGLISH BERRY TRIFLE

The towering trifles featured at every ball in *Bridgerton* may seem too intimidating to tackle, but a few modern shortcuts can help you create one in no time. Just make sure you prepare the gelatin dessert minutes before assembling the trifle. (Don't let it set first.)

SERVES 6

FOR THE CAKE

6 ounces pound or sponge cake

2 tablespoons sherry (optional)

1 (3-ounce) box strawberry gelatin dessert

2 cups fresh raspberries or strawberries

2 cups custard (recipe follows)

2 cups whipped cream

Fresh berries, for topping

Toasted almonds, for topping (optional)

FOR THE CUSTARD

4 cups whole milk

4 large eggs

½ cup sugar

¼ teaspoon salt

1 teaspoon pure vanilla extract

1. Line the bottom of the trifle bowl with the pound cake. Sprinkle the sherry, if using, over the cake and let it soak in for 5 minutes. Meanwhile, prepare a third of the gelatin mix according to the package's instructions.
2. Add a thick layer of berries to the dish, then slowly and evenly pour over them the liquid gelatin dessert. Transfer the dish to the refrigerator to set, 2–4 hours.
3. When the trifle has set, prepare the remaining two-thirds of the gelatin mix and pour the liquid over the trifle. Put it back in the refrigerator to set for 1–2 hours.
4. Meanwhile, make the custard. Preheat the oven to 350°F. In a small saucepan, heat the milk over medium-low heat until bubbles form at the edges, then remove it from the heat.
5. Whisk together the eggs, sugar, and salt in a large bowl until they are blended but not foamy. Very slowly stir in the milk, just a bit at a time, until incorporated, then stir in the vanilla.
6. Pour the custard through a fine-mesh sieve into a 6-cup baking dish. Place the baking dish in a large baking pan, transfer both to the oven, and fill the pan with very hot water to within ½ inch of the top of the baking dish.
7. Bake the custard until a knife inserted near the center comes out clean, 55–60 minutes. Remove the baking dish from water bath immediately and transfer it to a wire rack to cool for 30 minutes. Then transfer it to the refrigerator to cool completely.
8. Finish assembling the trifle: Spoon a thick layer of custard onto the gelatin, then add or pipe a thick layer of whipped cream on top and decorate with fresh fruit and nuts!

MIXED BERRY JELLY

When a Bridgerton decides to perpetuate a ruse, they pull out all the stops. That includes assembling a tea table overflowing with treats like this traditional English jelly. Although this recipe (like Violet's ruse) requires a bit of patience, you'll certainly enjoy the results!

SERVES 10–12

Nonstick cooking spray

2 cups mixed berries, cherries, and cranberries

5 (¼-ounce) envelopes unflavored powdered gelatin

7 cups cranberry juice cocktail, divided

1 cup sugar

1 (14-ounce) can sweetened condensed milk

Fresh berries, for serving

1. Coat a 10-cup Bundt pan or gelatin mold with cooking spray. Use a dry paper towel to evenly distribute the coating. Wash, dry, cut, and pit the fruit, then set it aside in the refrigerator.
2. Whisk together the gelatin and 1 cup of the juice in a medium bowl, then set it aside.
3. Add the sugar and the remaining 6 cups of juice to a medium saucepan over medium heat and stir until the sugar dissolves and the mixture just begins to simmer.
4. Remove the cranberry mixture from the heat and whisk in the gelatin mixture until well combined.
5. Reserve 3 cups of the cranberry gelatin in a large bowl and pour the rest into a second large bowl over an ice bath. Stir the gelatin frequently over 30 minutes to allow it to cool and thicken enough to hold the fruit. Then fold in the fruit.
6. Pour the gelatin-fruit mixture into the prepared mold and refrigerate it until set, about 2 hours.
7. Meanwhile, add the condensed milk to the reserved cranberry gelatin mixture and stir to combine. Let the mixture cool at room temperature until the refrigerated gelatin sets.
8. Once the fruit-filled gelatin is set, carefully and evenly pour the creamy gelatin mixture on top. (Turn the mold while you pour to help even things out.)
9. Put the mold back in the refrigerator to set for at least 4 hours, preferably overnight.
10. Once the dessert has set, remove it from the mold: Keeping the mold open-side up, place a platter on top. Carefully flip everything over. Give the dessert 2–3 minutes to drop. If it does not drop on its own, fill a sink with warm water and dip the outside of the mold in it for 10 seconds, then try again.
11. For a royal presentation, serve this elegant jelly on your best platter or stand, surrounded by fresh berries.

A BUNDT IN THE OVEN

A little cake leads to a lot of trouble for Marina, but it's just so hard to resist something this tasty. The cake is perfectly delightful (and packable for church baskets) on its own, but it's even sweeter with a vanilla glaze.

SERVES 8

FOR THE CAKE

Nonstick cooking spray

1 cup granulated sugar

½ cup unsalted butter, at room temperature

2 large eggs, at room temperature

¾ cup whole milk

2 teaspoons pure vanilla extract

2 cups all-purpose flour, plus approximately 1 tablespoon for the pan

2 teaspoons baking powder

¼ teaspoon salt

FOR THE GLAZE

2 cups powdered sugar

2 tablespoons whole milk

1 teaspoon lemon juice

½ teaspoon pure vanilla extract

1. Preheat the oven to 350°F and grease and flour a large Bundt pan.
2. To make the cake, using a hand or stand mixer, beat together the granulated sugar, butter, and eggs at medium speed until well combined. Reduce the speed to low and beat in the milk and vanilla, then return to medium speed and mix well.
3. Add the flour, baking powder, and salt and continue mixing until well combined and smooth, about 1 minute more.
4. Pour the batter into the prepared pan and bake for 30 minutes, or until a toothpick inserted into center comes out dry.
5. Use a knife to gently loosen the cake from the pan and turn it out onto a wire rack to cool completely.
6. Meanwhile, to make the glaze, combine the powdered sugar, milk, lemon juice, and vanilla in a medium bowl and stir until fully incorporated. Add more milk or powdered sugar to get a consistency that you can drizzle onto the cake without the glaze disappearing into it.

MINI CHOCOLATE BUNDT CAKES

Nothing goes on a *Bridgerton* table without a bit of fanfare, and these scrumptious little cakes are no exception. Using a mini fluted cake pan is an easy way to make this chocolate cake look as elegant as it tastes while brewed coffee deepens its flavor.

YIELDS 6

Nonstick cooking spray

1 cup all-purpose flour

½ teaspoon baking powder

¼ teaspoon baking soda

½ cup brewed coffee

½ cup unsalted butter

½ cup unsweetened cocoa powder

1 cup granulated sugar

½ teaspoon salt

1 large egg

1 teaspoon pure vanilla extract

½ cup full-fat Greek yogurt

Powdered sugar, for dusting

1. Preheat the oven to 350°F and grease a mini fluted cake pan (a pan with 6 fluted cavities) with cooking spray.
2. Combine the flour, baking powder, and baking soda in a medium bowl, and set it aside.
3. Add the coffee, butter, and cocoa powder to a large microwavable bowl and microwave it on high for 2–3 minutes, or until the butter melts.
4. Remove the mixture from the microwave and whisk in the granulated sugar and salt. Whisk in the egg until everything is well combined, then whisk in the vanilla and Greek yogurt until the mixture is smooth.
5. Add the flour mixture to the chocolate mixture and whisk until the ingredients are just combined and there are no lumps.
6. Spoon the batter evenly into the wells of the prepared pan, then lightly tap the pan on the counter to settle the batter.
7. Bake the mini Bundt cakes for 20–25 minutes, until a toothpick inserted in the centers comes out dry.
8. Let the cakes cool in the pan for 5 minutes before inverting the pan onto a wire rack to let the cakes cool completely. Dust the finished cakes with powdered sugar before placing them on an equally lovely table.

ROYAL RASPBERRY CAKE

No high-society ball could be complete without an elegant Charlotte Russe cake, which (like the queen herself) is, mercifully, less demanding than it seems. Follow the steps carefully, and you'll be amazed at how quickly this delicious cake comes together.

SERVES 8

8 ounces raspberries

¾ cup sugar, divided

2 (0.25-ounce) envelopes unflavored gelatin

5 ounces water

Zest of 1 medium lime

1¼ cups heavy whipping cream

24–26 ladyfingers

1. Wash the raspberries and set aside a handful for the top of the cake. Puree the rest in a blender. (If you like, strain the puree to remove the seeds.)
2. Whisk together a third of the puree, half the sugar, and the gelatin in a medium saucepan while the mixture comes to a boil over medium-high heat. Continue whisking for 1 minute more, until the sugar dissolves and the mixture thickens, then whisk in the rest of the puree. Remove the mixture from the heat and set it aside to cool.
3. Add the water, lime zest, and the remaining sugar to a small saucepan over medium heat. Stir until the sugar dissolves, then remove the syrup mixture from the heat and set it aside to cool.

4. Pour the cream into a large mixing bowl and use a hand mixer to whip it to stiff peaks. Set aside ¼ cup of the whipped cream. Using a spatula, gently fold in the puree just until the mousse is evenly pink and airy with no visible lumps.
5. Line an 8-inch round springform pan with parchment paper. One by one, soak the flat side of each ladyfinger in the syrup and place it against the rim, soaked side facing in. Soak and place the remaining ladyfingers on the bottom of the pan, soaked-side facing up. You should have a snug "crust."
6. Gently pour the mousse into the ladyfinger crust, smoothing it out evenly. Spread the remaining whipped cream over the top of the cake. Top with the reserved raspberries and let the cake set in the refrigerator for at least 4 hours or overnight.
7. When set, carefully remove the cake from the pan, peel off the parchment paper, and finish it off with an elegant ribbon before serving to your honored guests.

RICH, BUTTERY POUND CAKE

Will had to take a pounding to make it happen, but he'll be as rich as this buttery cake because of it. You'll need 12 eggs total for this recipe: 6 whole eggs and 6 additional yolks. But that just means you'll have egg whites to make another delectable recipe, like the Meringue Kisses on page 67.

SERVES 12

Nonstick cooking spray

3½ cups all-purpose flour, plus more for pans

2 cups unsalted butter, at room temperature

3½ cups sugar

6 large eggs

6 large egg yolks

1 tablespoon pure vanilla extract

1 teaspoon salt

1. Preheat the oven to 350°F and generously grease and flour two medium loaf pans, one 10-inch tube pan, or one 12-cup Bundt pan, shaking out any excess flour.

2. Use a hand or stand mixer to beat the butter in an extra-large bowl until it's creamy and smooth. Scrape down the sides of the bowl using a spatula, then add the sugar and beat until the ingredients are well combined, light, and fluffy, 1–2 minutes.

3. In a medium bowl, use a fork to combine the eggs, egg yolks, vanilla, and salt.

4. Slowly beat the egg mixture into the butter mixture with the mixer on low speed, allowing it to become fully incorporated before each addition. Scrape down the sides and bottom of the bowl, then increase the speed to medium-high and beat the mixture for another 1–2 minutes.

5. Reduce the speed to low and slowly add the flour to the batter, about ¼ cup at a time, until fully combined. Scrape down the sides and bottom of the bowl and continue mixing for 1 minute longer.

6. Spread the batter evenly into the prepared pan(s), using a spatula to smooth it.

7. Bake the pound cake for about 1 hour and 10 minutes, or until a toothpick inserted in the center of the thickest part comes out with a few moist crumbs.

8. Allow the cake to cool for at least 20 minutes in the pan, then use a knife inserted around the edges to release it onto a wire rack to cool completely before serving.

RUM-SOAKED RAKE CAKE

Much like Lord Featherington after losing a bet, this mouthwatering cake is overflowing with rum. Also like his lordship, this recipe uses shortcuts (cake and pudding mixes) to achieve its goals. Just keep in mind that the alcohol cooks out of the cake but is very apparent in the glaze.

SERVES 8–10

FOR THE CAKE

Nonstick cooking spray

1 (18½-ounce) box yellow cake mix

1 (3¾-ounce) box French vanilla instant
   pudding mix

4 large eggs, at room temperature

½ cup water

½ cup vegetable oil

½ cup dark rum

FOR THE RUM GLAZE

½ cup unsalted butter

¼ cup water

1 cup pure cane sugar

½ cup dark rum

1. Preheat the oven to 325°F and generously grease and flour a 10-inch Bundt pan.
2. To make the cake, in a large bowl using a hand or stand mixer, beat together the cake mix, pudding mix, eggs, water, oil, and rum until the batter is smooth.
3. Pour the batter into the prepared Bundt pan and bake for about 1 hour, until a toothpick inserted near the center comes out dry or with just a few moist crumbs.
4. Remove the cake from the oven and let it cool in the pan for 20 minutes, then invert it onto a wire rack to cool completely.
5. Meanwhile, make the glaze: Melt the butter in a heavy saucepan over medium heat, then whisk in the water and sugar. Bring the mixture to a light boil and let it cook, stirring constantly, for 5 minutes. Remove the glaze from the heat and stir in the rum. Allow it to cool slightly before using it on the cake.
6. Transfer the cooled cake to a rimmed serving platter. Using a fork or toothpick, prick the top of the cake all over to help it absorb the glaze.
7. Drizzle the glaze over the top and sides of the cake a bit at a time, allowing the cake to absorb the glaze each time, until you've used it up.
8. Serve slices of this scrumptious rum-soaked cake with a scoop of Sinful Vanilla Ice Cream (page 91).

VANILLA BUTTERCREAM CAKE

Violet Bridgerton may seem like just another eager mama on the surface, but she shepherds her sizeable brood with unparalleled joy and kindness. The beauty and simplicity of her love is the inspiration for this creamy vanilla cake.

SERVES 8

FOR THE CAKE

Nonstick cooking spray

3⅔ cups cake flour, spooned and leveled

1 teaspoon salt

2 teaspoons baking powder

¾ teaspoon baking soda

1½ cups unsalted butter,
    at room temperature

2 cups granulated sugar

3 large eggs, at room temperature

2 egg whites, at room temperature

1 tablespoon pure vanilla extract

1½ cups buttermilk, at room temperature

FOR THE FROSTING

1½ cups unsalted butter,
    at room temperature

6 cups powdered sugar

⅓ cup whole milk or heavy cream

1½ teaspoons pure vanilla extract

⅛ teaspoon salt

1 cup fresh blackberries

1. Preheat oven to 350°F and grease three 9-inch cake pans. Line each with parchment paper, then grease the parchment paper.

2. To make the cake, in a large bowl, whisk together the flour, salt, baking powder, and baking soda.

3. In a second bowl, using a hand or stand mixer fitted with a paddle or whisk attachment, cream the butter and granulated sugar on high speed for about 3 minutes. Scrape down the sides of the bowl using a spatula as needed.

4. Beat in the eggs, egg whites, and vanilla on high speed until combined, about 2 minutes. Scrape down the sides and, with the mixer on low speed, beat in the dry ingredients until just combined. Beat in the buttermilk until just combined, thick, and free of lumps.

5. Pour the batter evenly into the cake pans and bake them until a toothpick inserted into the center of each comes out dry, 23–26 minutes. Transfer the cakes, still in their pans, to a wire rack to cool completely.

6. Meanwhile, make the frosting: In a large bowl, use a hand or stand mixer to beat the butter on medium speed until creamy, about 2 minutes. Beat in the powdered sugar, milk, vanilla, and salt on low speed until combined, then increase the speed to high and beat for 2 minutes longer.

7. When the cakes are completely cool, use a large, serrated knife to slice a thin layer off the top of each to create flat surfaces. Add a small dollop of frosting to a plate or cake stand, then center the first round on it. Spread 1½ cups of the frosting over the top of the cake. Place the second round on top, then spread another 1½ cups of frosting on top. Finish with the final round and a layer of frosting over the entire cake.

8. Refrigerate the cake for at least 1 hour before topping it with blackberries (and any edible flowers you might like) and slicing it for guests.

NOT-JUST-A-GOOSEBERRY PIE

Is your pie just a pie, or is it a tasty pawn in an elaborate matchmaking scheme? When Lady Danbury and Violet Bridgerton get together, you can be sure that pie on your plate has plans. Luckily, the duke has very good taste in pie (among other things).

SERVES 8

FOR THE PIE

1 refrigerated piecrust

3 cups fresh gooseberries, divided

1½ cups granulated sugar

3 tablespoons quick-cooking tapioca

¼ teaspoon salt

FOR THE TOPPING

¾ cup all-purpose flour

3 tablespoons packed light brown sugar

½ teaspoons ground cinnamon

¼ teaspoon salt

5 tablespoons unsalted butter, melted

1. Preheat the oven to 450°F.
2. To make the pie, line a pie plate with the refrigerated crust.
3. Crush ½ cup of the gooseberries in a large bowl; add the granulated sugar, tapioca, and salt; and stir to combine. Stir in the rest of the whole gooseberries.
4. Transfer the mixture to a large saucepan over medium heat and cook, stirring frequently, until the pie filling thickens. Pour the pie filling into the crust and smooth the top.
5. To make the topping, whisk together the flour, brown sugar, cinnamon, and salt in a medium bowl. Add the melted butter and use your fingers to combine the mixture until it's crumbly.
6. Crumble the topping over the pie, then transfer it to the oven and bake for 10 minutes. Reduce the temperature to 350°F and bake for 30 minutes more, until the crust and topping are golden-brown. (If the topping is browning too quickly, cover the pie with aluminum foil.)
7. Serve the pie warm to any handsome and charming houseguests.

DRINKING CHOCOLATE

Both decadent and soothing, this time-honored treat requires just a bit more effort than your standard mix. But the best things in life often do (a lesson Daphne and Simon would do well to learn).

SERVES 4

3 cups whole milk

¼ cup sugar

2 tablespoons cocoa powder

1 cup semisweet chocolate chips

1 teaspoon pure vanilla extract

Whipped cream, for serving

1. Add the milk to a small saucepan and bring it to a simmer over medium heat. Whisk in the sugar and cocoa powder until smooth.
2. Stir in the chocolate chips and vanilla until melted and well combined, then remove the mixture from the heat.
3. Divide the cocoa among four mugs and top with a dollop of whipped cream. Enjoy hot with a freshly baked macaron (pages 68 and 70).

CHAPTER FOUR
DINNER-PARTY FARE

LAVENDER LAMB

Much like *Bridgerton* itself, this recipe is a colorful and flowery twist on a traditional dish. But for heaven's sake, don't pick the lavender yourself! Mrs. Colson can arrange that for you.

SERVES 6–8

FOR THE LAMB

¼ cup extra-virgin olive oil

¼ cup minced fresh rosemary, plus more
    for garnish

3 tablespoons minced fresh lavender leaves,
    plus more for garnish

4 medium cloves garlic, grated

1 (3½-pound) boneless leg of lamb

Kosher salt and freshly ground black pepper

FOR THE JAM

2 tablespoons extra-virgin olive oil

6 medium shallots, thinly sliced

½ cup pitted Medjool dates, thinly sliced

1 teaspoon honey

1 pinch salt

¼ cup apple cider vinegar

1. To make the lamb, in a small bowl, whisk together the olive oil, rosemary, lavender, and garlic.

2. Pat the lamb dry with paper towels and season it all over with salt and pepper. Rub the meat all over with the oil-herb mixture.

3. Place the lamb racks fat-side up on a large, rimmed baking sheet and let them stand for 1 hour.

4. Move a rack to the upper third of the oven and preheat the oven to 450°F. Transfer the baking sheet to the oven and roast the lamb for 15 minutes. Then turn the racks and roast for 10 minutes longer. The meat will be medium-rare.

5. Meanwhile, make the jam: Heat the olive oil in a medium saucepan over medium heat until shimmering. Add the shallots, dates, honey, and salt and cook, stirring occasionally, until the shallots are softened, about 7 minutes. Add the vinegar and continue cooking, stirring occasionally, until most of the liquid has evaporated and the jam is thick, 3–5 minutes. Remove the pan from the heat, season the jam with a pinch of salt, and let it cool.

6. Transfer the finished racks to a cutting board, stand them upright, and let them rest for 10 minutes. Slice the racks into chops, arrange them elegantly on a platter with a sprinkling of rosemary and lavender, and serve them with the shallot-date jam.

ROAST DUCK FIT FOR A DUKE

If you can keep your passions in check long enough to enjoy it, one small roast duck—brushed with a delicate orange sauce—can make a very romantic dinner for two. Just as Simon balances Daphne, a bit of crushed peppercorn balances the sweet citrus to create the perfect dish.

SERVES 2

1 (5-pound) duck

2 teaspoons grated orange zest

½ cup orange juice

1 tablespoon lemon juice

¼ cup currant jelly

⅛ teaspoon ground mustard

⅛ teaspoon kosher salt

¼ teaspoon crushed peppercorns

1 tablespoon cold water

1½ teaspoons cornstarch

1 orange, peeled and sectioned

1 tablespoon orange-flavored liqueur (optional)

1. Preheat the oven to 350°F.
2. Fasten the duck's neck skin to the back using skewers, fold the wings across the back with the tips touching, and place the duck, breast-side up, on the rack of a shallow roasting pan. Use a fork to pierce the skin all over, then loosely tie the legs to the tail (optional, to help it hold its shape during cooking). Insert a meat thermometer into the thickest part of the inner thigh muscle, being careful not to touch the bone.
3. Roast the duck, uncovered, for about 1 hour, then cover it with a tent of aluminum foil and continue roasting for 1½ hours longer. The duck is finished when the thermometer reads 180°F and the juices run clear when you cut into the center of the thigh.
4. Let the duck stand for 15 minutes while you prepare the sauce: Add the orange zest, orange and lemon juices, jelly, mustard, salt, and peppercorns to a 1-quart saucepan, stir, and bring the mixture to a boil. Stir in the water and cornstarch. Reduce the heat to medium and continue stirring and cooking until the sauce thickens and boils, then stir and cook for 1 minute longer.
5. Stir in the orange sections and liqueur, if using. Remove the sauce from the heat and brush about half of it over the duck. Serve the duck with the remaining sauce and enjoy while staring into the eyes of a handsome man.

MINI MEAT PIES

Delicious meat pies are just the beginning of local fare that makes its way to Clyvedon. To give yours that *Bridgerton* touch, use small cookie cutters to cut decorative flowers and leaves out of the puff pastry and place them on top of the crusts before brushing them with the egg wash.

YIELDS 16

FOR THE FILLING

3 tablespoons olive oil, divided

3 pounds chuck steak, cubed

2 medium onions, diced

3 medium cloves garlic, minced

2 tablespoons tomato paste

4 cups beef broth

1 cup dry red wine

2 dried bay leaves (or 3 fresh)

1½ teaspoons salt

2 teaspoons freshly ground black pepper

3 tablespoons cornstarch

¼ cup water

FOR THE CRUST

4 frozen piecrusts, thawed

3–4 sheets frozen puff pastry, thawed

1 egg yolk, lightly beaten

1. To make the filling, add 1 tablespoon of the oil to a large, heavy-bottomed pot over high heat. Sear half the beef at a time until the outside is lightly browned, and then set it aside.
2. Reduce the heat to medium-high and heat the remaining 2 tablespoons of olive oil. Add the onions and garlic and sauté until the onion is translucent, about 5 minutes.
3. Stir in the beef, tomato paste, broth, wine, bay leaves, salt, and pepper to combine.
4. Bring the mixture to a simmer, then reduce the heat to low so that it just bubbles. Continue cooking for 50–60 minutes, stirring occasionally, until the beef is very tender. Add water as needed if the mixture becomes too dry.
5. Near the end of the cooking time, combine the cornstarch and water in a small bowl and pour it into the pot. Stir to combine and continue cooking until the sauce thickens, about 5 minutes. Season again to taste.
6. Remove the pot from the heat and set it aside to let the filling cool and thicken. Remove and discard the bay leaves.
7. Preheat the oven to 350°F and spray sixteen individual pie tins with olive oil spray.
8. To make the crust, use a 4-inch round biscuit cutter to cut 16 rounds out of the piecrusts. Press the rounds into the tins and fill to the top with the beef filling.

9. Use a 3¼-inch round scone cutter to cut 16 rounds out of the puff pastry.

10. Place the puff-pastry rounds on top of the filling and gently press the edges to join the tops with the bottoms. Use a small knife to cut a few small slits in each pie top, then brush them all with the beaten egg.

11. Place the pies on a baking sheet and bake until they're a dark golden-brown, 20–25 minutes. Then remove them from the oven and allow them to rest for 5 minutes before transferring them to a wire rack to cool slightly before serving warm.

HERB-ROASTED TURKEY

If you need a dish to keep you as full as your dance card, this flavorful herb-roasted turkey will do just that. Baste often to keep the turkey as juicy as a Lady Whistledown missive.

SERVES 15

1 (15-pound) turkey, thawed if frozen
Kosher salt and freshly ground black pepper
1 medium onion, quartered
1 medium lemon, quartered
Several whole sprigs of herbs
    (sage, rosemary, and thyme)
10 tablespoons unsalted butter,
    at room temperature
2 teaspoons minced garlic
2 tablespoons finely chopped fresh sage leaves
1 tablespoon finely chopped fresh rosemary
2 tablespoons finely chopped fresh
    thyme leaves
¼ cup finely chopped fresh parsley leaves
3 cups chicken or turkey broth

1. Let the turkey stand at room temperature for 30 minutes, then tuck the turkey wings under the body of the bird. Preheat the oven to 450°F.
2. Season the cavity of the bird with salt and pepper, then place the onion, lemon, and whole herbs inside. Use kitchen twine to tie the turkey legs together in front of the cavity.
3. In a food processor, blend together the butter, garlic, sage, rosemary, thyme, parsley, a pinch of salt, and a pinch of pepper until smooth. Rub the herb butter under and over the skin of the turkey.
4. Place the turkey in a roasting pan, transfer to the oven, and roast for 45 minutes.
5. Warm the chicken broth in a medium saucepan over low heat. Reduce the oven temperature to 350°F and continue roasting for another 3 hours, basting the turkey with the warm broth every 30 minutes, until the internal temperature of the thickest part of the turkey thigh reaches 165°F on a meat thermometer. (Note: If the turkey starts getting too dark, cover it with aluminum foil.)
6. Let the turkey rest (loosely covered with foil) for 25 minutes before slicing and serving it.

BAKED HAM WITH PINEAPPLE

Pineapple was so pricey in Regency-era London that even high-society families would rent the fruit to decorate their tables rather than buying it to enjoy. So obviously, Queen Charlotte would want it front and center, adorning an especially tasty baked ham.

SERVES 20

1 (12-pound) bone-in ham

½ cup whole cloves

1 (20-ounce) can pineapple rings
  in heavy syrup

½ cup packed brown sugar

1 (20-ounce) bottle lemon-lime soda

1 (4-ounce) jar maraschino cherries

1. Preheat the oven to 325°F.
2. Place the ham in a roasting pan. Using a sharp paring knife, score the rind of the ham in a diamond pattern, then press a clove into the center of each diamond.
3. In a large bowl, combine the syrup from the pineapple rings, the brown sugar, and the lemon-lime soda. Pour this mixture over the whole surface of the ham.
4. Place the pineapple rings all over the ham in whatever arrangement you like. In the center of each ring, use a toothpick to secure a maraschino cherry.
5. Transfer the ham to the oven and bake, uncovered, for 4–5 hours, basting frequently with its own juices, until a meat thermometer inserted into the meat (but not to the bone) reads 160°F. If the pineapple gets dark too quickly, loosely cover the ham with aluminum foil. Remove the toothpicks before serving to awed guests.

ARTISTICALLY HERBED RED POTATOES

With the right recipe, Henry Granville might find just as much liberty in cooking as in art. These roasted reds have very few requirements. Just toss them in as much or as little of the ingredients as you like, and bake!

SERVES 4

Kosher salt

12 small red potatoes

Olive oil, to coat

Dried basil, to taste

Dried thyme, to taste

Dried rosemary, to taste

Freshly ground black pepper, to taste

1. Bring a large pot of salted water to a boil. Add the potatoes and boil them for 15 minutes, or until they are fork-tender. Pour off the water and set the potatoes aside.

2. Preheat the oven to 450°F. Grease a baking sheet with olive oil and spread the potatoes evenly over it.

3. Drizzle more olive oil over the potatoes, sprinkle them with the salt, herbs, and spices, and use your hands to coat the potatoes evenly.

4. Bake the herb-covered potatoes for 20 minutes, or until they're lightly browned and crisp.

COLORFUL CARROTS WITH THYME

Who's to say that dinnertime sides can't be as colorful and tasty as the treats served at teatime? In *Bridgerton*, only the most delectable dishes will do! The trick to getting these carrots perfectly roasted is to ensure they're all roughly the same size, cutting them down when necessary.

SERVES 6

2 pounds rainbow carrots with tops

2 tablespoons extra-virgin olive oil

¾ teaspoon garlic salt

Freshly ground black pepper

10–15 sprigs fresh thyme, divided

1. Place a rack in the center of the oven and preheat the oven to 425°F.
2. Scrub the carrots and trim their tops to 1 inch. Cut any larger carrots so that all are a similar size.
3. Toss the carrots with the olive oil to coat and place them on a large, rimmed baking sheet in a single layer. Evenly sprinkle the carrots with the garlic salt and pepper, then sprinkle the thyme sprigs over the sheet. Reserve a couple of sprigs for garnish.
4. Roast the carrots for 20–30 minutes, stirring every 10 minutes, until the carrots are very tender and starting to caramelize.
5. Transfer the carrots to a serving platter, remove the cooked thyme, and top with fresh thyme leaves from the reserved sprigs before serving.

BUTTERY ASPARAGUS WITH BRIE

Salty, sweet, buttery, and beautiful to look at—but enough about the Duke of Hastings. This recipe elevates asparagus to Grosvenor Square standards with creamy cheese, sweet-and-savory honey, and the light crunch of puff pastry.

SERVES 8

FOR THE PASTRIES

1 bunch asparagus, ends trimmed

1 tablespoon extra-virgin olive oil

Kosher salt and freshly ground black pepper

2 sheets frozen puff pastry, thawed

8 ounces Brie

1 large egg, beaten

Sesame seeds, for garnish

FOR THE THYME HONEY

¼ cup honey

2 tablespoons salted butter

1 tablespoon fresh thyme leaves

1. Preheat the oven to 375°F and line a baking sheet with parchment paper.
2. To make the pastries, toss the asparagus in the olive oil, salt, and pepper.
3. Gently roll the puff pastry out on a lightly floured surface and cut it into 8 squares.
4. Slice the Brie into 8 pieces. Place a piece of Brie on each square, followed by a handful of asparagus. Lift two opposite corners of each pastry square and fold them over the asparagus, one corner on top of the other.
5. Transfer the wrapped asparagus to the prepared baking sheet and brush each pastry with the beaten egg. Bake the pastries for 20–25 minutes, until golden brown.
6. Meanwhile, make the honey: Melt together the honey, butter, and thyme in a small saucepan over low heat.
7. Serve the pastries warm, drizzled with the thyme honey and sprinkled with sesame seeds.

WHITE SOUP

When soup is served at the finest dinner parties in the Square, it must be as exceptional the Season's own diamond. Like *Bridgerton*, this updated recipe offers a bit more flavor than the Regency classic.

SERVES 6

4 large parsnips, peeled

2 bulbs fennel, trimmed

2 tablespoons extra-virgin olive oil, plus more for drizzling

2 stalks celery, chopped

1 medium onion, chopped

2 teaspoons salt

½ teaspoon fennel seeds

4 cups water

1 whole bay leaf

1½ cups unsweetened almond milk

Crispy cooked bacon, chopped, for garnish (optional)

Grated Parmesan cheese, for garnish (optional)

1. Chop the parsnips and the fennel into 1-inch pieces. Heat the olive oil in a 3½-quart Dutch oven over medium-high heat. Add the parsnips, fennel, celery, onion, salt, and fennel seeds to the pot, reduce the heat to medium, and cook, stirring occasionally, for 6–8 minutes.

2. Stir in the water and the bay leaf and bring everything to a simmer, then reduce the heat to medium-low and cover with a lid. Let the soup simmer for 30 minutes, or until the vegetables are very soft. Turn off the heat, remove the bay leaf, and allow the soup to cool slightly.

3. Stir in the almond milk and use an immersion blender to puree the soup. (If you don't have an immersion blender, add the soup and almond milk to a blender in two batches.) Heat the soup over medium heat just to warm it through, then divide it among six bowls, each garnished with bacon and Parmesan.

BEST-DRESSED BAKED APPLES

Even apples must be dressed for the ball. Just as the women of *Bridgerton* don their finest clothing (and corsets), these baked apples are enveloped in mouthwatering puff pastry. For something a bit more traditional to the Regency era, add a splash (or two) of rum to the sauce after boiling.

SERVES 8

FOR THE APPLES

3 cups all-purpose flour

1 teaspoon kosher salt

1 cup shortening

⅓ cup cold water

Nonstick cooking spray

8 medium tart apples, peeled and cored

8 teaspoons unsalted butter

9 teaspoons cinnamon sugar, divided

FOR THE SAUCE

1½ cups packed brown sugar

1 cup water

½ cup unsalted butter, cubed

1. To make the apples, combine the flour and salt in a large bowl, then cut in the shortening until the mixture is crumbly. Slowly stir in the water until a ball of dough forms. Divide the dough into eight pieces, then cover it and move it to the refrigerator for at least 30 minutes.

2. Once the dough is easier to handle, preheat the oven to 350°F. Grease a 13 × 9-inch baking dish.

3. Roll each piece of dough out between two pieces of parchment paper to create 7-inch squares. Place an apple in the middle of each square, and then place 1 teaspoon of butter and 1 teaspoon of cinnamon sugar in the center of each apple.

4. Bring up the corners of the square to the center, pinching them to create a seal. (You can wet the corners with a bit of water to help them stay put.) Add the wrapped apples to the prepared baking dish and sprinkle them with the remaining 1 teaspoon of cinnamon sugar.

5. To make the sauce, add the brown sugar, water, and butter to a large saucepan and bring just to a boil, stirring until everything is blended.

6. Pour the sauce over the apples in the baking dish. Transfer them to the oven and bake the wrapped apples for 50–55 minutes, basting occasionally with the sauce, until the apples are tender when pierced with a knife and the pastry is golden brown.

PEARS POACHED IN SPICED WINE

Every event in the *ton* is made better by an abundance of alcohol—in the glasses, in the dinners, and certainly in the guests! These pears are soaked in a syrup for an especially warm and welcoming flavor.

SERVES 4

2 cups dry red wine

¼ cup + 1 tablespoon sugar

Juice of 1 medium orange

1 (1 × 3-inch) strip orange zest

1 cinnamon stick

2 whole cloves

4 large pears, firm and ripe

1. Combine the wine, sugar, orange juice, orange zest, cinnamon stick, and cloves in a large saucepan over medium-high heat. Bring the mixture to a boil, then reduce the heat and let the liquid simmer for 5 minutes.

2. Meanwhile, gently peel the pears, leaving the stem intact. (For easier peeling, blanch the pears first.) Slice ½ inch off the bottom of the pears to create a flat surface. Gently place the pears in the poaching liquid, cover the pan, and let the liquid simmer for 15–20 minutes, turning the pears every 5 minutes, until the pears are cooked but still firm.

3. Remove the saucepan from the heat, uncover the pan, and let the pears cool. Then re-cover the pan, transfer it to the refrigerator, and chill the pears for at least 3 hours or up to 24 hours, turning them occasionally for even coloring.

4. Gently remove the pears from the liquid and allow them to come to room temperature.

5. Meanwhile, make the syrup. Transfer the saucepan to the stove and reduce the liquid by about half by cooking it over medium-high heat for 15 minutes. Remove the pan from the heat and let the syrup come to room temperature.

6. Place the pears on a serving dish and drizzle each with about 2 tablespoons of the syrup.

CHAPTER FIVE

REGENCY COCKTAILS

BRANDY DAISY WITH ORGEAT

Looking for a drink that will make you feel like you stepped into Lady Danbury's "den of iniquity"? This libation is light and bubbly but packs a punch (much like Daphne herself).

SERVES 1

2 ounces brandy

2 dashes rum

2–3 dashes Curaçao liqueur

3–4 dashes orgeat or simple syrup

Juice of ½ medium lemon

1 ounce soda water

1. Pour the brandy, rum, Curaçao, orgeat, and lemon juice into a cocktail shaker filled with ice and shake well.
2. Strain the mixture into a chilled cocktail glass and top it with the soda water.

LEMON-MINT CORDIAL COCKTAIL

Swap that small glass of lemonade for one of the Regency era's "restorative" favorites: the cordial-infused cocktail. This sweet drink is the ideal refreshment when you need a break from an overbearing older brother or an overzealous suitor.

SERVES 16

Zest and juice of 4 medium lemons

4 cups sugar

1 ounce tartaric acid

5 cups boiling water

Gin or vodka, for serving

Fresh mint, for garnish

1. Add the lemon zest, lemon juice, sugar, and tartaric acid to a large bowl.
2. Pour the boiling water over the ingredients, and stir until the sugar has completely dissolved.
3. Strain the mixture and pour it into a sterilized glass bottle or jar with a lid. (Store the unopened bottle in the pantry. Once opened, store it in the refrigerator.)
4. When ready for a drink, add one part cordial to three parts gin or vodka, garnish with some fresh mint, and enjoy a moment of respite while you sip!

FRUIT-INFUSED RATAFIA

Ratafia is a traditional Regency-era drink and also the preferred beverage for distracting older brothers. It takes three weeks to make, which gives you plenty of time to get your matchmaking plans in order.

SERVES 10

1 quart brandy

½ (750 ml) bottle champagne

½ cup gin

¼ cup sugar

2 medium oranges, sliced

2 cups cherries, pitted and crushed

2 cups blackberries

1 dash cinnamon

1 dash nutmeg

1 teaspoon dried rosemary

3 whole cloves, bruised

¼ cup crushed almonds

1. Combine all ingredients in a 1-gallon glass container and shake well.
2. Store the container in a dark place at room temperature for 3 weeks, shaking it once each week.
3. After 3 weeks, strain the liquid through cheesecloth, squeezing the cloth to release any extra liquid.
4. Transfer the strained ratafia to smaller containers to store or gift, or simply fill the glasses of thirsty guests!

MARRIAGE MARKET PUNCH

Nothing helps soothe the nerves during a new London Season like a delightful (and strongly spiked) champagne punch! Rum (or brandy) gives this flavorful beverage an extra kick to encourage strong attachments.

SERVES 20

5 cups 100 percent juice cranberry beverage

2 (750 ml) bottles very dry champagne

2 cups apple cider

1½ cups diet ginger ale

1½ cups dark rum or brandy

1 (5-pound) bag of ice

2 oranges, thinly sliced into rounds

1 cup fresh cranberries

1. Chill the juice, champagne, cider, ginger ale, and rum in the refrigerator before mixing the punch.
2. Pour the ice into a large punch bowl. Stir in the chilled juice, champagne, cider, ginger ale, and rum.
3. Top the bowl or individual cups with orange slices and a smattering of fresh cranberries before serving.

MULLED WINE

If you want to keep up with the *ton*, you can add a bit of brandy or your favorite liqueur to this traditional Regency drink. Just don't waste your best bottle—this isn't a duel. The spices will overpower any subtle notes in the alcohol.

SERVES 4–6

1 (750-ml) bottle dry red wine

1 orange, sliced into rounds, plus more for garnish

8 whole cloves

2 cinnamon sticks, plus more for garnish

2 whole star anise, plus more for garnish

2–4 tablespoons sugar or honey

¼ cup brandy (optional)

1. Combine the wine, orange slices, cloves, cinnamon sticks, star anise, 2 tablespoons sugar or honey, and brandy (if using) in a large saucepan over medium-high heat.
2. Allow the mixture to cook just until it reaches a low simmer, then reduce the heat to low, cover the pan, and let the mixture simmer gently for at least 15 minutes or up to 3 hours.
3. Using a fine-mesh sieve, strain the wine and discard the cooked orange slices, cloves, cinnamon sticks, and star anise.
4. Serve the wine warm, in heatproof mugs, topped with fresh orange slices, cinnamon sticks, and star anise for garnish.

CONVERSION CHARTS

METRIC AND IMPERIAL CONVERSIONS
(These conversions are rounded for convenience)

Ingredient	Cups/Tablespoons/Teaspoons	Ounces	Grams/Milliliters
Butter	1 cup/ 16 tablespoons/ 2 sticks	8 ounces	230 grams
Cheese, shredded	1 cup	4 ounces	110 grams
Cornstarch	1 tablespoon	0.3 ounce	8 grams
Cream cheese	1 tablespoon	0.5 ounce	14.5 grams
Flour, all-purpose	1 cup/1 tablespoon	4.5 ounces/0.3 ounce	125 grams/8 grams
Flour, whole wheat	1 cup	4 ounces	120 grams
Fruit, dried	1 cup	4 ounces	120 grams
Fruits or veggies, chopped	1 cup	5 to 7 ounces	145 to 200 grams
Fruits or veggies, pureed	1 cup	8.5 ounces	245 grams
Honey, maple syrup, or corn syrup	1 tablespoon	0.75 ounce	20 grams
Liquids: cream, milk, water, or juice	1 cup	8 fluid ounces	240 milliliters
Oats	1 cup	5.5 ounces	150 grams
Salt	1 teaspoon	0.2 ounce	6 grams
Spices: cinnamon, cloves, ginger, or nutmeg (ground)	1 teaspoon	0.2 ounce	5 milliliters
Sugar, brown, firmly packed	1 cup	7 ounces	200 grams
Sugar, white	1 cup/1 tablespoon	7 ounces/0.5 ounce	200 grams/12.5 grams
Pure vanilla extract	1 teaspoon	0.2 ounce	4 grams

OVEN TEMPERATURES

Temperature	Celsius	Gas Mark
225°	110°	¼
250°	120°	½
275°	140°	1
300°	150°	2
325°	160°	3
350°	180°	4
375°	190°	5
400°	200°	6
425°	220°	7
450°	230°	8

INDEX